CHAMPIONSHIP SOCCER

CHAMPIONSHIP SOCCER

Antonio Carlos Pecorari

TATU and KEVIN CROW
with Sigi Schmid

CB
CONTEMPORARY
BOOKS
CHICAGO · NEW YORK

Library of Congress Cataloging-in-Publication Data

Pecorari, Antonio Carlos.
    Championship soccer / Tatu and Kevin Crow with Sigi Schmid.
       p.   cm.
    ISBN 0-8092-4614-7
    1. Soccer.   I. Crow, Kevin.   II. Schmid, Sigi.   III. Title.
  GV943.P36   1988
  796.334'2—dc19   88-39276
                                            CIP

Tatu photos by Phil Stephens
Kevin Crow photos by Essy Ghavameddini

Published by Contemporary Books, Inc.
180 North Michigan Avenue, Chicago, Illinois 60601
Manufactured in the United States of America
Library of Congress Catalog Card Number: 88-39276
International Standard Book Number: 0-8092-4614-7

Published simultaneously in Canada by Beaverbooks, Ltd.
195 Allstate Parkway, Valleywood Business Park
Markham, Ontario L3R 4T8 Canada

CONTENTS

PREFACE   vii

1   INTRODUCTION   1

2   A WORD ABOUT SOCCER TECHNIQUES   3

3   PASSING   5

4   RECEIVING (BALL CONTROL)   17

5   DRIBBLING   33

6   SHOOTING   51

7   HEADING   61

8   A LESSON ON BASIC SOCCER TACTICS   69

9   DEFENSIVE PLAY   71

10   OFFENSIVE PLAY   81

11   DEFENDERS   87

12   MIDFIELDERS   93

13   FORWARDS   97

14   GOALKEEPER   103

15   SPECIFIC FUNDAMENTALS FOR INDOOR SOCCER   117

16   SOCCER REQUIREMENTS   123

PREFACE

Working on a book with Kevin Crow and Tatu was a tremendous experience. The book is a reflection and combination of ideas based on their experiences. It would have been easy for Tatu and Kevin to fill many more pages, but a conclusion had to come somewhere.

Kevin is an American soccer player who has come through the American soccer player system. He was a high school and club team player in Pleasanton, California, and went on to an All-America career at San Diego State. In 1983 he joined the San Diego Sockers and has played on the Socker's MISL championship teams of 1984, 1985, 1986 and 1988. Kevin has been a four-time MISL All-Star (1985, 1986, 1987, and 1988), an NASL all-star (1984), and the MISL Defender of the Year in 1985 and 1988. Also, Kevin has found time to represent the United States internationally. He was a member of the 1984 and 1988 Olympic teams and has been a U.S. national team member since 1983.

Tatu, a native of Mairinque, Brazil, has been called the best indoor soccer player in the world. In 1987, he was the MISL's regular season player and Championship Series Most Valuable Player, leading the Dallas Sidekicks to the league title. Tatu signed his first professional outdoor soccer contract at age 17 for the famed Sao Paulo after the team won the 1980 and 1981 Brazilian championship and finished second in 1982.

Tatu left Brazil to play indoor and outdoor soccer for the Tampa Bay Rowdies and he is now "the most marketable soccer player in the U.S. since Pele" according to *Sports Illustrated*. Tatu is expected to dominate the MISL offensively for many years—as he did during the 1986–87 season with 111 points, 73 goals, nine hat tricks and 10 game-winning goals. With his celebrated ritual of throwing his game jersey into the stands after his goals, Tatu has gained thousands of fans across the country.

Tatu and Kevin are both great soccer ambassadors. Kevin won the 1987 MISL Community Service Award and has been a leader in the growth of American youth soccer. Tatu spends much of his time working with children, coaches an under-16 soccer team during the summer, and is planning to open his own summer soccer camp.

Combining the insights of these two players allows the reader to get a defensive and offensive view of the game. *Championship Soccer* combines the quick, dynamic high scoring and flair of Tatu with the smooth, powerful, and intelligent play of Kevin Crow. With every page I either learned something new or was able to confirm an idea I already held. You will find the concepts presented in this book helpful; players of every size can have success in soccer, as these two show. This book represents the best soccer played in America. Enjoy.

Sigi Schmid
Head Soccer Coach
UCLA

ACKNOWLEDGMENTS

Tatu and Kevin Crow thank Pat Brennan and John C. Boggs of Garvey Marketing Group; Kevin O'Keefe and Steve Horowitz of ProServ; Essy Ghavameddini, photographer, San Diego Sockers; Billy Phillips of the Dallas Sidekicks and Bill Nattal of Mitre; and Phil Stephens, photographer, Dallas Sidekicks.

The authors also wish to thank American Airlines and its division manager in sales promotions/Los Angeles, Leo Loane. American Airlines coordinated the necessary flights for Kevin and Tatu in their writing of the book.

American Airlines
Something special in the air.

CHAMPIONSHIP SOCCER

1

INTRODUCTION

Soccer is the world's most popular sport and is attracting more participants in the United States each day. The basis for this popularity is that the size of the player is unimportant, the equipment is inexpensive, and every player plays offense as well as defense. The most popular professional soccer league in America is the Major Indoor Soccer League, and indoor soccer is gaining worldwide recognition through many international tournaments. The World Cup, the most prominent outdoor soccer tournament in the world (played every four years) will be held in the U.S. in 1994. In this book we want to support the sport by offering you, the player or coach, some facts, exercises, tips, and hints that will help you further enjoy the game. Playing soccer is about having fun. As a coach, you need to make sure that players enjoy practice while still accomplishing your goals. As a player, just enjoy the game; approach it with a fun attitude.

A WORD TO COACHES

You need to be patient and communicate with individual players and the team as a group. Bring a positive attitude to practice, for players perform better in that environment. If players are young, move them around to different positions. Players should be given the opportunity to try all positions before a coach sets the lineup.

At practice, work with the ball as much as possible and keep the time organized and efficient. Idle time causes kids to lose concentration. Plan your practice in advance and keep exercises simple, fun, and competitive. If you can demonstrate or find someone else to demonstrate for your team, you will improve their learning. Keep talking to a minimum and do not begin teaching tactics until age 13 or so. Tactics are of no use if the players have not mastered techniques. Having fun and being positive are important, but that does not mean you should not use discipline when it is needed.

When teaching a new skill to young players, follow a consistent progression. Each drill should start simply, then move to incorporate the pressure of an opponent. By gradually increasing intensity, you allow

1

success but are always pushing the individual or group to the fullest. Conditions in practice are used to adapt any practice exercise to the skill level of your team. Examples of conditions are the number of touches, the size of the area, or defensive pressure. Remember that you as the coach know your team, so adapt the exercises to your team so they are challenging and allow success.

A WORD TO PLAYERS

Individual players can do so much to enhance their own ability. Practicing on team practice days alone is not enough. Train with friends or on your own. A tennis or plastic ball is good enough to play soccer with. A game of soccer-tennis or soccer-volleyball is different but develops skill. Juggling is a fun individual exercise. Remember to use juggling as an aid only; do not make it the goal of your learning.

Dedication is the key to success. When you are in the learning stage, do not get discouraged, for you learn from mistakes. But if you enjoy the sport of soccer and want to become very good, you need to be dedicated. Listen to your coach, do what he or she says, and practice on your own. Organize your friends and get together for pickup games. As you get older, prepare well for games by getting the proper amount of sleep and adopting good eating habits.

Many talented players have not achieved success because they are not dedicated. Each player, young or old, can work on improving his or her game. Dedication *can* make you a better player.

Together, player and coach can learn in the upcoming chapters how to work individually and in groups to improve skills. Basic principles of defense and offense are explained, as are individual positions. Have fun, work hard, and enjoy your time playing soccer.

2

A WORD ABOUT SOCCER TECHNIQUES

The foundation for any successful soccer player is technique. Acquiring knowledge of the fundamental aspects of basic skills allows the player to control the ball—and therefore the game. Players with poor fundamentals find themselves reacting to the game rather than dictating to the game. The key is to control the ball; do not let the ball control you.

Soccer skills can be divided into six areas:

1. Passing
2. Receiving (ball control)
3. Dribbling
4. Shooting
5. Heading
6. Goalkeeping (catching, diving, throwing, punting)

Learning the skills in the order of this list is recommended (goalkeeping skills will be dealt with separately). An easy way to remember this order for skill learning is that it reflects the way a game progresses.

The kickoff is a pass, followed by receiv-

ing the ball, then a dribble, followed by more passing and receiving, and ending with a shot on goal.

You can practice soccer skills alone or with friends. For practicing alone, use that often-forgotten friend, the wall. A wall can serve as a passing partner, backstop, and even something to rest against when you get tired.

As you can see, with a wall around, you never have to practice alone. You do, however, need to follow some golden rules when practicing, whether alone or with friends.

Always concentrate on what you are doing. Soccer players need to concentrate for the entire game. In the 1987 Pan-Am game between the United States and Argentina, the United States seemingly lost its concentration and gave up two goals in three minutes, thereby wasting 87 minutes of hard work.

The second golden rule is to keep your eye on the ball whenever you strike it. It is tough to kick or pass the ball well when you do not see it.

3

Third, communicate with your teammates; if you're a coach, talk to your players. It will help them and you become better.

Finally, look around when playing. Keep your vision sharp and aware. Knowing where opponents and teammates are will make you a better passer, dribbler, and scorer.

Now you are ready to acquire some skills.

Here is a key to the figures located throughout this book.

Path of ball   Running without ball   Dribbling

3

PASSING

Learning how to pass well at an early age will eventually give young players the space necessary to learn dribbling in games and be successful at it. And good passing skills can keep you in the game for a long time. Kaz Deyna, who played with Kevin Crow from 1983 to 1987, was able to play until age 39 because of his highly advanced passing ability. Passing is the thread that weaves a game together and the way you share with and reward your teammates. A good pass makes it as easy as possible for a teammate to control the ball and make his or her next move. An assist is often more difficult for a player to make than the goal that follows.

There are different types of passes, but all good passes have two things in common:

1. Pace (weight)
2. Accuracy

The pace or weight of your pass should be hard enough to reach your teammate in a reasonably short amount of time, but not so hard that it becomes uncontrollable. On the other hand, the pass should not be light or slow enough that it could be easily intercepted by your opponent.

Remember, accuracy does not always mean the ball goes straight to your teammate. Sometimes the proper pass is played into the area your fellow player is running toward (**Figure 3-1**).

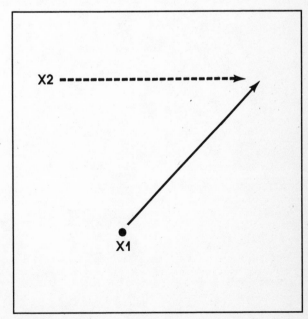

Figure 3-1.

5

The different types of passes are distinguished by the point of impact with your foot. There are the inside-of-foot pass *(Photo 3–1)*, outside-of-foot pass *(3–2)*, instep drive *(3–3)*, chip pass *(3–4)*, and back-heel pass *(3–5)*.

All these passing techniques can also be used for shooting. Whether indoors or outdoors, passing requires the same technique. The difference is primarily distance; also, because the indoor fields are smaller, long chip passes are not used often.

In this chapter we will talk about the inside-of-foot pass, the outside-of-foot pass, and the back-heel pass. In the chapters on shooting we will deal with the instep drive and chip pass.

Photo 3-1

Photo 3-2

Photo 3-3

Photo 3-4

Photo 3-5

INSIDE-OF-FOOT PASS

The inside-of-foot pass is the most commonly used pass in soccer. Generally, this pass is used for short distances (1–20 yards) and is accurate because you are striking the ball with the largest surface area of your foot (3–1).

The proper technique requires that you strike the ball with your knee over the ball, the ankle in a locked position (heel down, toe pulled up), and your leg bent slightly at the knee. Your nonkicking foot is pointed in the direction you are passing

Photo 3-6

Photo 3-7

Photo 3-8

Photo 3-9

the ball, and the leg is bent at the knee to evenly balance your weight. The nonkicking foot is next to the ball (3-6 and 3-7). The follow-through is straight (3-8 and 3-9). Remember, keep your eyes on the ball when you are making contact.

Figures 3-2 to 3-7 show beginning exercises for practicing the inside-of-foot pass.

Two players pass the ball to each other. The nonactive player has his legs spread apart. The passing player tries to pass it through the other player's legs. The distance between players should be 10-15 yards at the beginning stage.

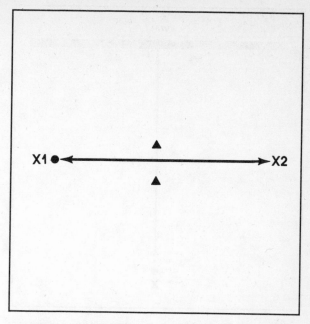

Figure 3-2. Pass the ball back and forth between two cones. Initially, the players should stop the ball, then pass. As skill improves, pass without stopping the ball.

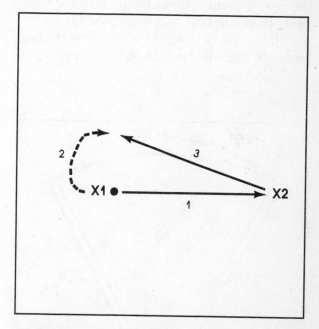

Figure 3-3. Player X1 passes the ball, then moves back (jogging backward) five yards or so, then moves forward to meet the pass and repeat. After 10-15 passes, the players change roles. For the forward, this drill teaches the player to meet the ball before it is intercepted by a defender. For the defender, the drill teaches the player how to make the interception.

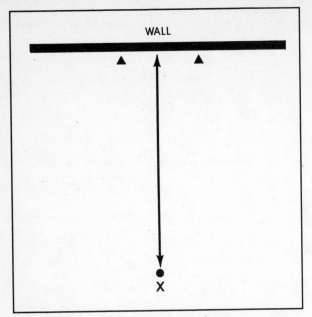

Figure 3-4. You can practice on your own by using your friend, the wall. Practicing with a wall is great preparation for using indoor dasher boards. Using two cones, pass the ball accurately between the cones from a distance of 10 yards. At first, stop the ball when it comes back to you; later, pass it again when it returns. Increase the distance as skill improves.

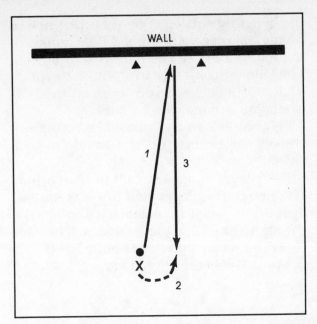

Figure 3-5. Pass the ball forward, jog back five yards, then come forward to meet the ball again. Repeat.

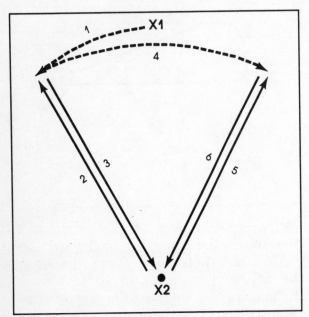

Figure 3-6. Player X1 moves from one side to the other, returning the pass. After 10–15 passes the players change roles.

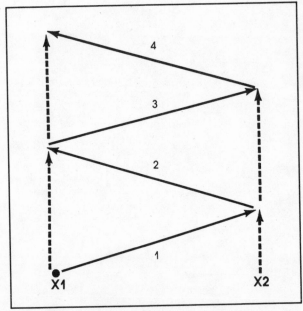

Figure 3-7. The players advance up the field, passing the ball back and forth.

OUTSIDE-OF-FOOT PASS

The outside-of-foot pass allows you to pass the ball from your normal running stride *(3–10)*.

Executing this pass requires that your ankle be locked, with your foot pointed down and slightly in. The knee of the kicking leg is over the ball and bent. The standing leg is bent at the knee for balance, and the foot is pointed away from the direction of the pass and farther away from the ball than in the inside-of-foot pass *(3–11 to 3–14)*.

The exercises in **Figures 3-5** and **3-6** can also be used for practicing the outside-of-foot pass. The wall can also be used, as in **Figure 3-4**.

Photo 3-10

Photo 3-11

Photo 3-12

Photo 3-13

Photo 3-14

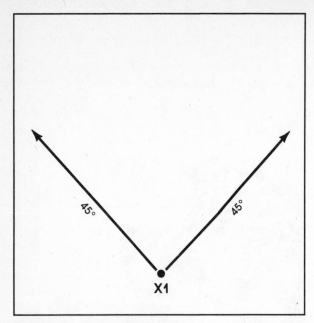

Figure 3-8. This pass is very effective when passing the ball at a 45-degree angle.

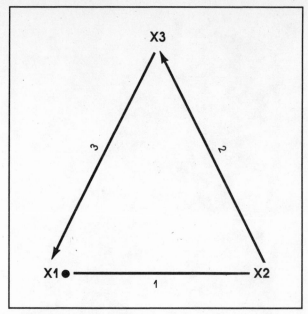

Figure 3-9. Three players form a triangle and pass the ball to each other. It is important for the passing player to move so that the pass travels away at a 45-degree angle.

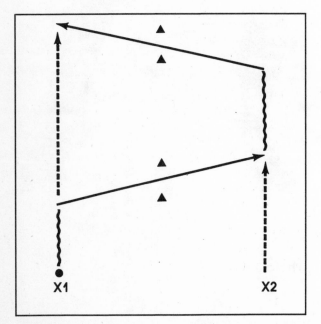

Figures 3-9 to 3-10 show beginning exercises for practicing the outside-of-foot pass.

Figure 3-10. Outside-of-foot passes can be practiced between two players. Players dribble the ball and pass the ball through "gates" marked by cones. Continue this exercise for the length of the field. Remember, the distance of the pass and the size of the gates are determined by your skill level.

BACK-HEEL PASS

Although this pass seems fancy, it is really simple and useful. There are two types: the simple back-heel pass and the crossover back-heel pass. While the back-heel is more simple to execute, the crossover is the much more effective pass.

The simple back-heel pass requires that you place the nonkickng foot slightly ahead of the ball and to the outside of the ball (3–15). The kicking foot is brought over the ball, and a gentle backswing propels the pass. Again, the ankle is locked, toes up, and the knees are bent for balance.

In the crossover back-heel pass, notice the knee of the standing leg is bent for balance (3–16). When heeling the ball with the right foot, the ball lies just outside the left foot. The leg of the kicking foot is bent at the knee, and the ankle is locked, toe up. A gentle backswing is all that is needed to pass the ball. The same type of exercises used for practicing the two preceding passes can be used for this pass also.

Once a player has learned to pass the ball, beginning with a stationary ball and progressing to an active player and ball, you can use keep-away games at practice. These games are excellent for practicing all types of passes. The size of the teams depends on skill levels. See **Figure 3-11** for examples of keep-away games.

Photo 3-15

Photo 3-16

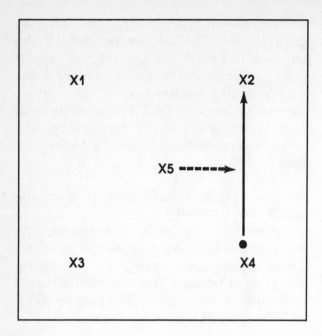

Figure 3-11. Four-on-one. Four players keep the ball away from one player in a grid area. The size of the grid varies; the better the skill, the smaller the grid. Variations of this setup include three-on-one, five-on-two (which is very popular with professional teams), six-on-two, and eight-on-four.

In all keep-away games the first pass is free; it cannot be intercepted. The player who makes the bad pass replaces the central player. You can restrict the number of ball contacts (touches) you allow the outside players. For example, professional teams play five-on-two with one touch. Younger players (under age 12) can play the same game with unlimited touches.

4

RECEIVING
(BALL CONTROL)

When learning how to pass, you also have to learn to stop the ball. Stopping the ball involves receiving and ball control. However, when you receive the ball, you do not always want to stop it.

Receiving the ball means preparing the ball for your next move. If your next move requires a stationary ball, you stop the ball as in the beginning passing exercises (see Chapter 3). But later, as you become more skillful, you control the ball by gently controlling and playing the ball in one motion into a space away from the opponent. You will save time and touches by knowing where you are going to go with the ball when you receive the pass.

The ball is your friend, so treat it well. Soccer is a game of time and space. Ball control is crucial to a good player because he or she can maximize time and space by controlling the ball early and properly. Effective ball control is achieved using these three principles:

1. Keeping your eyes on the ball through the point of impact

2. Relaxing the part of the body that is meeting the ball

3. Cushioning the ball by bending your knees to soften the impact

Any and every part of the body can be used to control the ball. Generally, the following types of ball control are used most often:

- Instep *(Photo 4–1)*
- Inside *(4–2)* or outside of foot
- Sole *(4–3)*
- Thigh *(4–4)*
- Chesting a high ball *(4–5)*
- Chesting bouncing ball *(4–6)*
- Head *(4–7)*

It is best to control the ball with the part of your body that is closest to the ground if you have a choice. Pressure from an opponent often allows no choice. But if you have time, using your thigh rather than your chest, for example, gives you more time on the ball, since the shorter distance

17

allows the ball to get to the ground sooner. In addition, go to the ball rather than wait for it to come to you whenever possible. This allows you more time on the ball to execute your next move and prevents a defender from intercepting the pass.

Photo 4-2

Photo 4-1

Photo 4-3

Photo 4-4

Photo 4-5

Photo 4-6

Photo 4-7

METHODS OF BALL CONTROL

Instep

As a ball-receiving surface, the instep is used primarily to cushion the ball. The key is balance, with your standing leg slightly bent at the knee. The receiving leg is also bent to allow you to cushion the ball *(4–8)*. With practice, you can actually catch and hold the ball on the instep *(4–9)*.

Start with your leg slightly extended forward and at the time of impact, relax your leg by gently moving it in the direction the ball is traveling. This action will bring the ball to a stop. Imagine catching an egg; if you hold your hands rigid, the egg will crack as you catch it. However, by moving with the egg in the direction that it is traveling, you soften the blow and avoid cracking it. It is important to remember that as you cushion the ball, your ankle is in a locked position *(4–10 to 4–13)*.

Photo 4-8

Photo 4-9

Photo 4-10

Photo 4-11

Photo 4-12

Photo 4-13

Inside or Outside of Foot

The inside and outside of the foot can also be used to control balls coming out of the air. Controlling the ball with the inside or outside of your foot allows you to use the largest surface area of the foot. This control can be accomplished in two ways. One is to cushion the ball *(4–14 to 4–16)*. The second is to use wedge control. The basis of this manner of receiving a ball is using the ground and wedging the ball between the ground and your foot. As the ball hits the ground, your foot comes over the ball just as it is about to bounce up so that it rebounds into space for you to execute your next move *(4–17 to 4–20)*.

Photo 4-15

Photo 4-14

Photo 4-16

Photo 4-17

Photo 4-18

Photo 4-19

Photo 4-20

Sole

The sole of the foot is used to control rolling balls as well as to wedge-control air balls. When receiving a rolling ball, it is important to lock your ankle, toes bent up and heel low to the ground. Bend the receiving leg slightly so you have a controlling surface that does not allow the ball to slip under your foot (4–21).

Thigh

Young players often neglect using the thigh, chest, and head to control the ball. Receiving a ball by using these areas generally saves time and allows you to retain your balance.

Your standing leg is bent for balance. As it prepares to receive the ball, the trapping leg is bent, with the thigh coming parallel

Photo 4-21

Photo 4-22

to the ground *(4–22)*. You want the ball to land on the middle of the thigh, halfway between knee and hip *(4–23)*. To cushion the ball at the point of impact, gently pull your leg back, with the thigh finishing perpendicular to the ground *(4–24)*. Beginners should realize that it is not always possible to control the ball on the first touch. Everyone should strive for one-touch control, but it is not necessarily a bad trap if two touches are used.

Photo 4-23

Photo 4-24

Chest

A well-executed chest trap of an air ball is one of the most beautiful sights in soccer. Teaching this to young players is difficult only because initially they are stiff in their execution, and therefore the ball hits their body awkwardly.

In Brazil, players are taught to trap with the chest or head by first catching the ball. The ball is thrown at their chest, and the young players catch it *(4–25)*. Next, they pretend to catch it by opening up their arms and letting the ball hit their chest *(4–26)*. Opening the arms with the arms bent at the elbows and held above the waist teaches balance. In addition, having your arms in this position keeps opponents away and allows you more time and space to execute your next move. A cushioning effect is achieved by bringing your arms back forward after the ball passes down toward the ground *(4–27)*. A player can turn his chest to direct the trap to where he wants to move next.

Controlling a bouncing ball with your chest is similar to using a wedge control. You want to lean your body over the ball so that when the ball strikes your chest it returns to the ground in the direction you are moving. *(4–28 to 4–30)*.

Photo 4-25

Photo 4-26

Photo 4-28

Photo 4-27

Photo 4-29

Head

Controlling the ball with the head can be taught in the same manner as a chest trap. At first, catch the ball. Later, open your arms and allow the ball to pass through. Bending at the knees will allow your legs to absorb the impact *(4–31 and 4–32)*.

Photo 4-30

Photo 4-31

BALL CONTROL EXERCISES

Always begin with stationary exercises; next advance to movement, then pressure of an opponent. Playing in pairs and simply passing the ball back and forth is a good way to begin. Putting players in larger groups allows for passing, trapping, and moving. When trapping air balls initially, beginning players should serve the ball with their hands.

Exercises with more activity can be added as the players improve, and first-time passing, where the player uses only one touch rather than two to control and pass the ball, should be required.

Use your creativity to create many more exercises. As skill improves, keep-away games (as described in Chapter 3) best combine passing and ball control with gamelike pressure. The important part is to execute the skills properly; do not be satisfied with sloppy fundamentals.

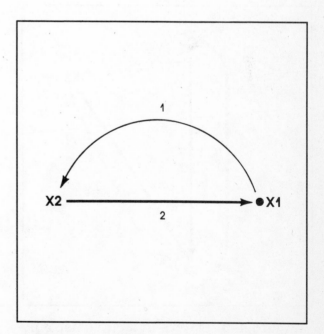

Figure 4-1. Player X1 serves the ball in the air to player X2, who controls it, then passes it back. After a set number of serves, they change roles. Also practice touching the ball off the player's head two or three times before passing it back.

Photo 4-32

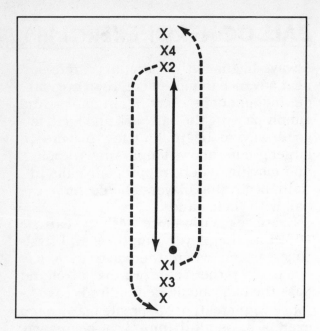

Figure 4-2. Player X1 passes to X2 and follows the pass by running to the end of X2's line. X2 controls the ball and passes it to X3, then runs to the back of that line, and so on.

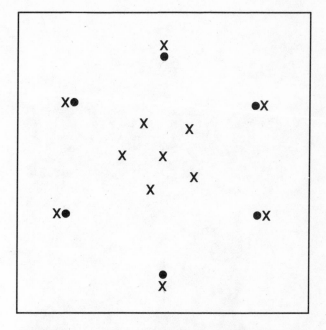

Figure 4-4. Each player on the outside has a ball. Each inside player demands a pass from an outside player. The inside player controls the ball, then passes it back. After completing this, the inside player runs toward and demands a pass from a different outside player. Do not allow players to run in a circle, since they do not run in circles in games. All inside players work at the same time; after a set interval, they change roles with the outside players. This structure can also be used for air balls.

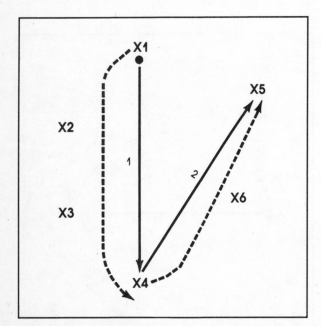

Figure 4-3. Players in a circle use only one ball (two balls if players are skilled). Pass the ball and follow the pass. The player receives the ball, controls it, passes to another teammate, and follows the pass.

5

DRIBBLING

Dribbling is often considered a lost art form in soccer. The variations and feints that you can learn are limited only by your imagination. In this chapter you will learn some basic, common skills, as well as some feints.

ELEMENTS OF DRIBBLING

Flexibility

In order to be an effective dribbler, you must achieve flexibility. Your ankles, knees, hips, waist, and upper body all must move with suppleness to be truly effective. Running a slalom in and out of corner flags rather than cones forces upper body and waist flexibility. This slalom should be done first without the ball. In Brazil, this is used as a basic teaching method for upper body swerve. Setting the flags in tight formations makes a player bound and twist between flags. After body swerve has been achieved, the same slalom can be done with the ball.

To guide the ball in and out of the flags, you should tap the ball lightly with the inside of your left foot or the outside of the right foot to move to the right; and guide the ball with the outside of the left foot or the inside of the right to move to the left. As you improve, and your ball-handling skills become more efficient, increase your speed. Make sure to maintain control of the ball at all times.

Ankle dexterity can be aided by various types of ball tapping and ball control movements. In the first exercise, be sure to bend your knees and work on your toes *(Photos 5-1 to 5-3)*.

In the next exercise, roll the ball back with the sole of your foot, allowing the foot to roll back off the ball with your toes down. The ball should then be in front of your instep *(5-4 to 5-6)*. Tap the ball forward and use the sole of the other foot to stop the ball. Repeat the process.

Touch the ball alternately with the inside and outside of the same foot as you dribble forward *(5-7 and 5-8)*. Body swerve is used here.

Photo 5-1

Photo 5-2

Photo 5-3

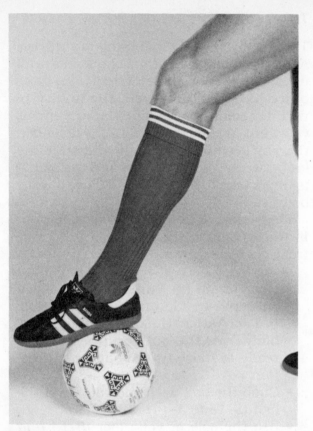

Photo 5-4

Photo 5-5

Photo 5-6

Photo 5-7

Photo 5-8

Turns

The next element of dribbling is surprise. A quick turn, acceleration, or a feint are all used to "fake out" a defender. Once flexibility has been achieved, the ability to turn becomes important. In all the turns, you want to turn away from the defender, thereby keeping your body and standing leg between your opponent and the ball. It is important to keep the ball close to your body.

The easiest turn if you're a young player is to go back in the direction you came from; there are several ways to do this:

- Chop or cut the ball back toward you with the inside of your foot *(5–9 to 5–11)*. Notice the player's balance, body over the ball, and bent knees ready to move in the opposite direction.
- Chop the ball with the outside of the foot *(5–12 to 5–14)*.
- Use the sole of your foot *(5–15 and 5–16)*.
- Cut the ball back behind your standing leg. The standing leg should be away from the ball to allow execution of this turn *(5–17 to 5–19)*.

Photo 5-9

Photo 5-10

Photo 5-11

Photo 5-12

Photo 5-13

Photo 5-14

Photo 5-15

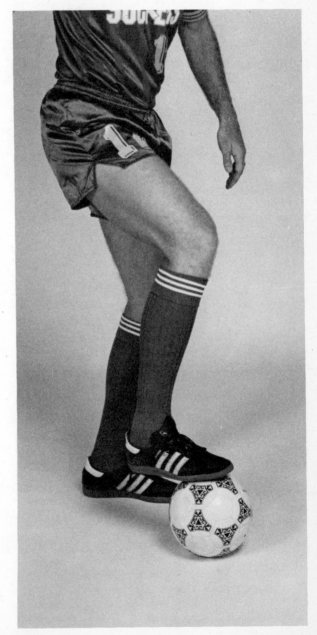

Photo 5-16

Photo 5-17

Photo 5-18

Photo 5-19

Another effective change of direction is a 90-degree turn. This turn can be accomplished by rolling the ball back toward your body and your standing foot with your toe. Then, with the inside of the standing foot, gently push the ball off in the other direction *(5–20 to 5–22)*.

Photo 5-21

Photo 5-20

Photo 5-22

With the next move turn in the same direction as the foot you are using. Pivot on your standing leg and pull the ball back with the toe. After pivoting, gently push the ball forward with the inside of the same foot (5–23 to 5–25).

To practice an alternative form of this exercise, use the outside of the same foot to gently push the ball forward.

A key point when dribbling, executing a feint, or controlling the ball is that when the sole of the foot is used you are actually using the toe area. This allows better ball feeling, balance, and quickness.

Many exercises can be used to improve basic dribbling skills:

- Dribble through a line of cones that are approximately five yards apart.
- Dribble in a 30-by-30-yard or 20-by-20-yard area and execute certain turns on command without running into one another.
- Randomly set up cones in a grid and dribble, staying in the grid but not hitting any cones.
- In a grid with, for example, 10 players with a ball and two without, the players without a ball must steal a ball from one of the other players. The players with balls must dribble, staying within the grid and avoiding loss of the ball. Once a player loses the ball, he or she becomes the hunter and tries to steal a ball.

Photo 5-23

Photo 5-24

Photo 5-25

Feints

We have looked at body flexibility and turning as two key elements of dribbling. Besides teaching basic ball handling, turns can also be effective feints. A fake is worthless, however, if it is not followed by a change of speed. Stopping quickly can be as effective as acceleration in performing an effective feint.

A basic feint combines swerve with acceleration. Dropping your shoulder in one direction and leaning your body in the same direction will convince the opponent that is where you want to go. Then bring the opposite foot (if faking to the left, use the right foot and vice versa) behind and to the inside of the ball. Shift your body weight and firmly push the ball forward with the outside of the foot at a 45-degree angle. Then accelerate *(5–26 to 5–28)*.

After mastering this first move, you can develop the scissor feint. As you drop your shoulder to the left, for example, simultaneously pass your left foot in front of or over the ball. Again, as in the earlier feint, the right foot is brought behind and to the inside of the ball. Then push the ball forward firmly at a 45-degree angle and accelerate *(5–29 to 5–32)*.

The double scissor is exactly what it sounds like. After making the initial fake with the left foot, make the same fake with the right; follow that by using the left foot to complete the feint as described above.

The double scissor confuses the defender. An attacking player should always be unpredictable to a defender. Sometimes use the obvious move; other times, use the unexpected one. Surprise is the best weapon a dribbler has.

Photo 5-26

Photo 5-27

Photo 5-28

Photo 5-29

Photo 5-30

Photo 5-31

Photo 5-32

The last feint is a double hit. As you approach the opponent to begin the feint, lean your body in one direction (for example, to the right) and gently touch the ball with the inside of your left foot, moving the ball to the right. Almost immediately after you touch the ball, shift your body weight to the left and tap the ball firmly forward (45 degrees) with the inside of your right foot (5–33 to 5–35).

Photo 5-34

Photo 5-33

Photo 5-35

6

SHOOTING

Scoring goals by shooting can be divided into two skill areas. The first is scoring tactics, and the second is shooting technique.

SCORING TACTICS

Scoring requires not only good shooting ability but also good, clear thinking. The following are keys to successful scoring:

1. Do not overpower the ball. Accuracy outweighs power, and often "passing" the ball into the goal is an effective technique *(Photo 6–1)*.
2. Surprise the goalkeeper. This gives you, the attacker, a great advantage; unexpected shots are often successful.
3. Recognize an opportunity to shoot. Many young players think they have to completely beat a defender before they can shoot; however, space is all you need. Sometimes as little as six

Photo 6-1

51

Photo 6-2

inches is enough to get the shot off *(6–2)*.

4. Allow for a margin of error. If you hit your shot well, you will score. Even if you make a slight error, your shot can still land in the corner; however, beginning players should not aim directly for corners. Players should aim slightly to the left or right of the goalkeeper. Also, do not be overly concerned with the goalkeeper.

5. Shoot for the far post when approaching the goal from an angle. Especially in an indoor game, for post-shots that go wide will result in rebounds off the boards that then become goals *(6–3)*.

6. The closer you are to the goal, the less power is needed. A quick release is most important.

7. Take chances. You will not score if you do not shoot. When you think you have an opportunity, let the shot fly; you might surprise yourself—and the goalkeeper.

SHOOTING TECHNIQUES

Now that you know when to shoot, let's discuss shooting technique. Imagine that the soccer ball looks like a face (**Figure 6-1**). Striking the ball on the ears will result in a spinning shot. Hitting the nose will keep the ball low, and striking the mouth will cause the shot to rise.

The primary shot used is the instep drive. It is important to keep your ankle locked, toe down; the point of impact should be along your shoelaces. Keep your knee over the ball and hit the ball on the "nose" to keep it down. Your standing leg is next to the ball, pointing in the direction of the shot. As you strike the ball, propel yourself up on your toes (and, in many cases, off the ground) with your standing leg to increase velocity *(6–4 to 6–6)*.

Figure 6-1

Photo 6-3

Photo 6-4

Photo 6-5

Photo 6-6

The chip shot is also hit with the instep; the foot is not bent down in a severe angle, though the ankle is still locked. The point of impact is just behind the big toe and slightly ahead of the laces. Hit the ball in the "mouth" so it gains height. The standing leg is a little farther from the ball than in the instep drive *(6–7 and 6–8)*.

Photo 6-7

Photo 6-8

The curving shot, also called a *banana shot* for obvious reasons, is an exciting shot to watch. It can make goalkeepers look foolish and the impossible look possible. The banana shot is often used to get around a defender. You can use either the outside or the inside of the foot to hit the ball's "ears," which will result in a curving shot. When hitting the ball with the inside of the foot, lock the ankle, pull the toe up slightly, and let the ball strike your foot just behind the big toe *(6–9)*. Remember, hit the "ear" of the ball and follow through. This will give the ball spin. You can achieve spin using the outside of the foot by locking the ankle, toe bent down, and turning the foot slightly to the inside *(6–10)*. The standing leg should be away from the ball.

Another shot that is used sometimes, especially indoors, is toeing the ball. This shot is proper only if you have no time to make a backswing or can barely reach the ball. It is most often used at close range. Use it if you have to, but when you can, choose another shot.

Scoring a goal directly out of the air often creates soccer legends. The famous Pelé scissor kicks are the most difficult of volley shots. The toughest aspect of shooting volleys is keeping the ball on target. Getting your knee over the ball will help keep the shot low. Drop your shoulder to force your leg up and your knee over the ball; your leg should be almost parallel to the ground. Your standing leg is bent at the knee for balance *(6–11 and 6–12)*. Strike the ball by snapping your leg forward below the knee to generate enough power. Swinging your whole leg will not be

Photo 6-9

Photo 6-10

Photo 6-11

Photo 6-12

effective. Notice in *6–13* how the striking leg is bent at the knee so the knee is over the ball to keep the shot on target. When taking a shot, a player needs to bend forward whenever possible. Leaning backward often results in the ball going over the goal.

An important element of the above shots is power. The speed of a shot is generated for the most part from the snap, or extending your leg, below the knee as you contact the ball *(6–14)*.

Photo 6-13

Photo 6-14

SHOOTING EXERCISES

Shooting exercises should be progressive in nature, just like all the other skills. Begin with stationary exercises.

1. Two players punt the ball back and forth. Watch the spin on the ball; your toe should be down to give the ball a forward rotation. If the ball has backspin, your toe is incorrectly pointed up.
2. Two players shoot the ball back and forth. Use whatever type of shot you want, but stop the ball before executing the shot.
3. Divide into groups of three (**Figure 6-2**). Player X2 is the goalkeeper between two cones. Player X1 takes a shot; then X3 takes a shot. After two minutes, change goalkeepers. By using this setup you avoid a lot of ball chasing and wasted time. At first, the players should stop the ball before

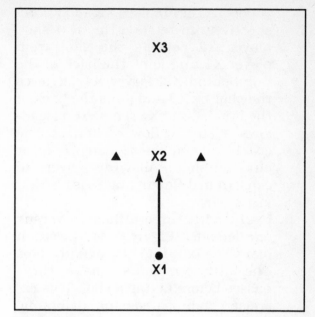

Figure 6-2

shooting. Later, the players strike a moving ball.
4. Players X1 and X3 dribble forward and shoot on goal (**Figure 6-3**). After

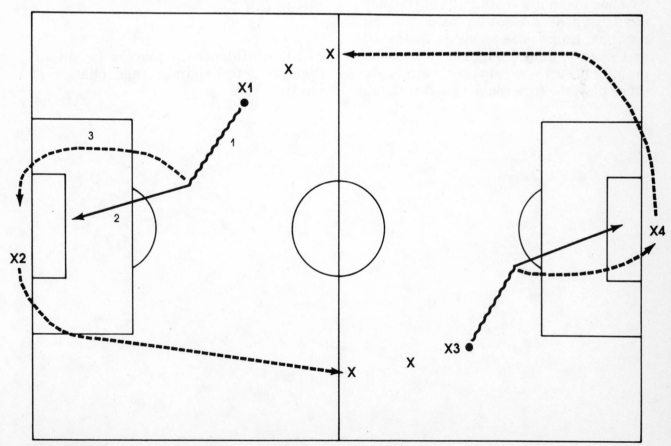

Figure 6-3

shooting, they replace X2 and X4, respectively, to retrieve the next shot. Player X2 collects the shot from player X1 and joins the back of the line behind X3. Player X4 retrieves the shot by X3 and joins the back of the line behind X1. This exercise allows a steady flow of action. The coach can emphasize instep, chip, or curving shots. Allowing players to come from different angles is also advised.

5. Begin with three attackers versus one defender (**Figure 6-4**). The coach plays the ball into the penalty box. The attackers must make three passes before taking a shot. This exercise combines passing, dribbling, and shooting, just like the game. After an interval of two minutes, bring in a new group or change roles. Once the skill level improves, add another defender.

Shooting is an art, but sometimes coaches make it too difficult for the players. Most goals are scored inside the penalty box. Emphasize shooting in the 10-to-18-yard range. Remember, shooting practice is meant to help the forwards and other players score goals. Coaches should

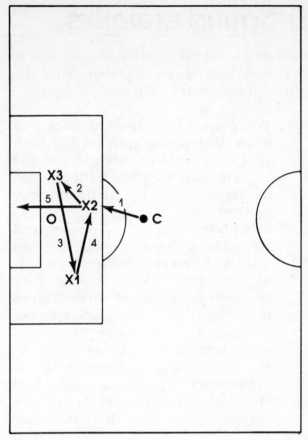

Figure 6-4

instill confidence in players by giving them a better-than-average chance of scoring.

7

HEADING

Heading is unique to soccer and is an important skill to master for the outdoor game.

In Chapter 4 a technique for teaching heading was described. The same approach applies when teaching heading as a means to propel the ball. The coach should throw the ball at a young player's head and have the player catch it. The player opens up his or her arms to let the ball pass through and simultaneously brings the head forward, keeping the eyes open and mouth closed, jutting the chin forward *(Photos 7–1 to 7–3)*. Keeping the eyes open is important because even though everyone blinks at the time of impact, the player should watch the ball as long as possible. Also, to avoid injury, learn to keep the tongue unexposed when heading. The player strikes the ball with the head, where the hairline begins. Remember, *you* hit the *ball*; do not let the ball hit you.

The power for heading is generated from the lower back. Great headers are arched like a bow in preparation for heading the ball *(7–4)*.

Photo 7-1

Photo 7-2

Photo 7-4

Photo 7-3

Heading can be divided into defensive and offensive skills. The objective in defensive heading is to head the ball high and wide, away from the offensive pressure. You should get slightly underneath the ball to head it up *(7–5)*.

When heading offensively, whether passing or attempting a goal, you want to head the ball down, by jumping and waiting for the ball to drop before meeting it. When scoring, remember that the goal is only 8 feet high, so by heading the ball toward the ground you'll be sure to make a direct hit *(7–6)*. When passing, heading the ball down will give you more control over the pass and your teammate will be able to gain control of the ball quickly.

By far the most exciting type of heading is the diving header. When well executed, the player becomes a human torpedo propelling his or her body forward into the incoming ball *(7–7 to 7–10)*. To execute a diving header, keep your eye on the ball, strike with your forehead, and use your hands to break your fall. Prior to propelling yourself forward, compact your body by bending at the knees and waist to put yourself in line with the ball's path. Then push yourself forward using your legs. Whether the result is a great goal or a dramatic clearance, the diving header is always exciting.

Photo 7-5

Photo 7-6

Photo 7-7

Photo 7-8

Photo 7-9

Photo 7-10

EXERCISES

A basic heading exercise is the progression beginning with catching the ball, described earlier in this chapter. Here are some more exercises for practicing heading.

- A player holds the ball in his or her hands at forehead level and gently heads the ball back into his or her hands *(7–11 to 7–13)*. This exercise helps players overcome their fear of heading. Remember, when heading is done properly, it does not hurt.
- One player serves the ball underhanded to a kneeling player. The kneeling player heads the ball back *(7–14)*. Kneeling forces the player to arch his or her back to generate power. In this exercise, the catching technique can be used before asking players to head the ball.

Photo 7-12

Photo 7-11

Photo 7-13

Photo 7-14

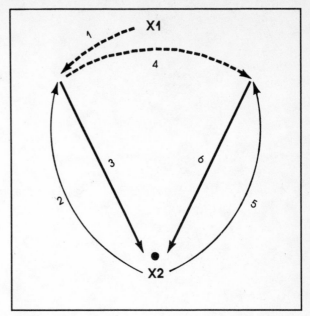

Figure 7-1

- One player serves the ball to a standing player, who heads the ball back.
- Do the preceding exercise, except now the heading player must jump to head the ball. Remember, jump early so you can arch your back to get good power on the ball when heading.
- The player works from side to side, heading the ball. This exercise introduces movement prior to heading (**Figure 7-1**).
- Player X1 jogs forward to head the ball, served by X4, into the goal. After X1 heads, player X2 starts forward to head the ball from X3 (**Figure 7-2**). Change servers at intervals and have players change lines to practice heading in opposite directions.

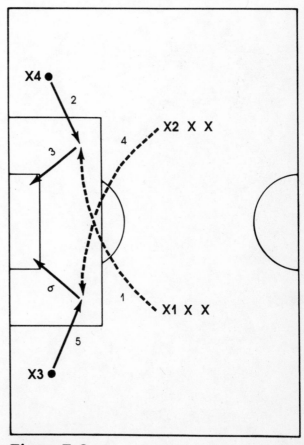

Figure 7-2

8

A LESSON ON BASIC SOCCER TACTICS

Skills are the fundamental base for a soccer player. You cannot employ tactics to any meaningful advantage without the skill that allows execution. For example, the opponent might have a weak outside fullback, and your tactic is to try to challenge this fullback. Completing the task requires dribbling skills, crossing, and shooting ability. If you possess none of these fundamentals, you cannot make use of tactics. Therefore, as a young player, practice the basics and learn the fundamentals so that you are able to take advantage of tactics.

All players are responsible for two types of tactics: general tactics and specific tactics. General tactics are the fundamentals of individual and team play that create time, space, or numerical advantage. Specific tactics are a planned approach to exploit a specific opponent's weakness and take advantage of your strengths.

In the upcoming chapters we will look at general tactics as they apply to individuals. First are general defensive and offensive tactics; then we will look at positions—goalkeeper, defenders, midfielders, and forwards.

Systems of play is something both coaches and players discuss often. Remember, players make the system work—not the other way around. In describing systems, the first number represents defenders, the second number represents midfielders, and the third number represents forwards. A 4–4–2 therefore means four defenders, four midfielders, and two forwards. The numbers are a nice way to identify a system, but do not rely on them as the key to making a team better.

Most professional outdoor teams now play either a 4–4–2, a 4–3–3, or a 3–5–2, with the 4–3–3 being the least used. What this tells us is that most teams play with only two forwards. As a result, these players must be versatile and very mobile. A big, tall forward is not necessary in a two-striker system. Some of the best forwards are skilled, quick, mobile, and versatile, though not tall (Tatu is 5'7").

Photo 8-1

Indoor teams play in either a 2-1-2 or a 2-2-1 system. One forward is high, and again there is a strong desire to have quick, mobile forwards *(8-1)*.

The key: players make the system work. Let's turn now to individual tactics.

9

DEFENSIVE PLAY

Good defensive play is invaluable to the success of a team. The defensive player must be determined, courageous, and hardworking but also have the ability, skill, and vision to start the team's attack. To be a successful team, all players need to be good defenders; soccer requires that everyone play defense *and* offense. So even if you are a forward, this chapter applies to you, just as it does to a fullback.

PATIENCE

You must always know where you are on the field. Delaying an opponent and waiting for help from teammates is a sign of a good defender (Photo 9–1). As a defender, you are waiting for the attacking player's mistake. If you "dive" into a tackle on a good player, he or she will react to your move and easily go around you.

Naturally, if your opponent is about to shoot at goal, more extreme measures than waiting are called for. Nevertheless, patience is a great quality to develop.

The defender, to use patience properly,

should force a player to a less dangerous part of the field, usually the outside. Know your opponent's strengths and tendencies and look for a key that will predict his or her next move. Watch the ball, not the player's head or upper body fakes; the player cannot score or pass without the ball. Stay balanced on the balls of your feet and force the attacker to move in the direction you want (9–2). Be prepared for a change of pace. Finally, jockey the attacker and make him or her react to you by pretending to come at the ball and then jumping back; this way the attacker must concentrate on the ball and cannot calmly look for a passing or dribbling option.

Practicing defense against a friend can help you learn patience, as can the dribbling exercises.

MARKING OR COVERING AN OPPONENT

A defender first wants to deny the opponent the ball, which can be accomplished

Photo 9-1

Photo 9-2

Photo 9-3

by intercepting, an often-overlooked ability. If the opponent does receive the ball, do not allow this player to turn with it. Make the opponent pass it back; that way you keep the ball and your opponent in front of you (**Figure 9-1**). Remember, always block your opponent from the goal side of the ball *(9–3)*.

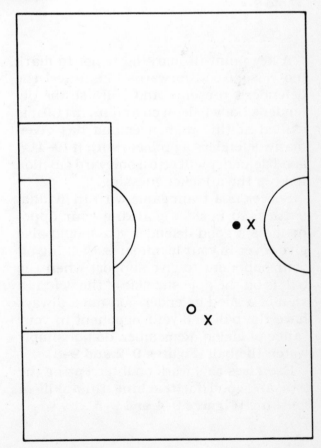

Figure 9-1. Notice the defensive player is between the opponent, X, and the goal.

Photo 9-4

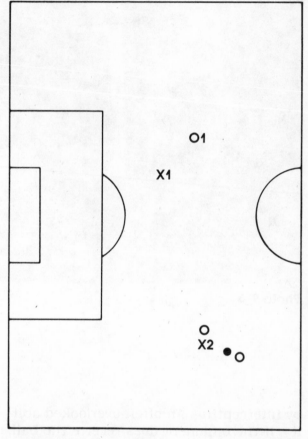

Figure 9-2. Notice how X1 is marking O1 but also is providing cover for X2. Both O1 and the ball are in X1's range of vision.

A key point in marking is not to mark too close. Good forwards like to feel the defender's presence and will use the defender's body to lean on and turn. (Tatu is skilled at this maneuver and has given many defenders a problem with it *(9–4)*. A good defender will give a one-yard cushion to keep the attacker guessing.

Soccer is a team game with individual battles, so besides marking your opponent, as a good defender you should also give cover to your teammates. Backing off your opponent to give support when the ball is on the opposite side of the field is a sign of a good defender. You must always have the ball and your opponent in your range of vision. Remember, do not simply watch the ball (**Figures 9-2 and 9-3**).

Exercises that work on intercepting the ball are good for teaching this skill of marking (**Figures 9-4 and 9-5**).

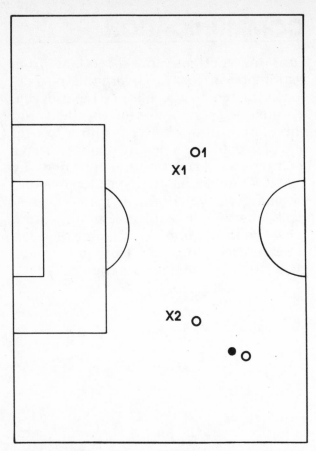

Figure 9-3. X1 in this example is marking but not providing cover.

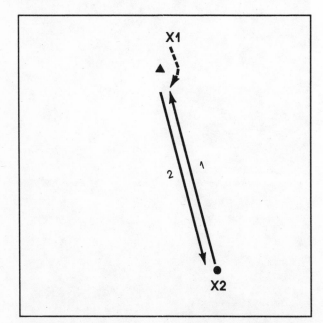

Figure 9-4. X1 steps around the cone to intercept the ball. As skill improves, use a passive attacker instead of a cone.

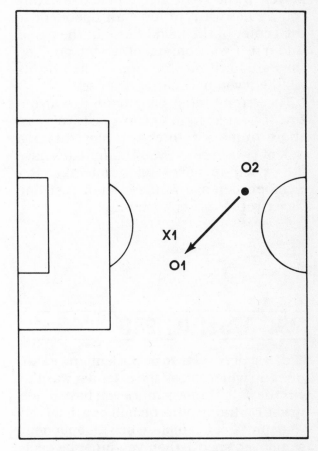

Figure 9-5. X1 is marking O1, who has a ball played in to player O1 from O2. If the defender can intercept the ball, fine. If not, he or she must mark and try to stop O1 from scoring. This exercise emphasizes one-on-one defense.

SOCCER INTELLIGENCE

Learn the strengths and weaknesses of your teammates and the opponents. Play to the strengths of your teammates and to the weaknesses of your opponents.

If your opponent is left-footed, force this player to the right if possible. (Generally, you do not want to force an opponent to the center of the field.) Early in the game, find out if your opponent is fast, good on the ball, hardworking, and so on. All this will help you play better defense.

The strengths of your team are also a key. If your teammates are fast, you can afford to mark tighter and maybe take a risk or two, because your teammates have the speed to cover up a mistake. Remember, defense is more than just one player versus an opponent.

COMMUNICATION

Oral instructions and directions from teammates are critical in organizing a defense. Listen to the players behind you, because they see more of the field and therefore are in a better position to help you play defense. A helpful shout can save a player a lot of running and prevent many a goal. When double-teaming an opponent, be smart: you will be forced to make quick decisions which require communication with your teammate. Communication often means asking your teammates questions such as "Who are you marking?"

AGGRESSIVENESS

The first point was to be patient and calm, to set up when you as the defender want to win the ball. However, once you have made up your mind to win the ball or are forced to commit (for example, when an opponent is about to shoot), then you must be decisive and quick. A defender who hesitates is generally beaten *(9–5)*.

Photo 9-5

DETERMINATION, OR THE WILL TO GET THE BALL

The mental determination and belief that you will win the ball are keys to being a solid defender. Everyone *wants* to get the ball; however, only a select few are *determined* to get it *(9–6)*.

When marking an opponent, bend your knees a little and concentrate on that player's moves; be ready to make whatever move is necessary.

Photo 9-6

TACKLING

Tackling is the art of taking the ball away, or winning the ball, from your opponent in a one-on-one confrontation. As a tackler, you will have to be patient, skilled at marking and covering, aggressive, and, above all, determined. A good tackler will not only win the ball, but keep possession of it.

A block tackle is made with the broad surface of the foot (inside); the knees of both the tackling leg and the standing leg are bent for balance. The upper body is over the ball for strength. After initial con-

Photo 9-7

Photo 9-8

tact, rolling your foot up the ball often allows you to roll the ball over the attacker's foot.

Often a player will try to beat you on speed. Before using a slide tackle, you can successfully tackle and win the ball by placing your body between the opponent and the ball (9–7). The ball must be within playing distance, and you must use speed and determination to win the ball cleanly.

The slide tackle is more complicated but no less efficient. The player should approach the attacker from either side, staying slightly behind. The player should slide into the ball at the moment after opponent has kicked the ball forward, at the point the ball is farthest from the ball carrier. Ideally, the foot nearest the attacker should strike the ball for the tackle.

The slide tackle is a last resort because if you miss you'll wind up sitting on the ground, no longer a part of your team's defense (9–8).

Timing is essential to a good tackle. Generally, it is best to tackle with the foot nearest the attacker; that way, if the opponent falls on your foot, it is flat on the ground, and you will avoid injury.

All one-on-one exercises teach tackling skills and defense.

NEVER RELAX WHILE THE BALL IS IN PLAY

Usually during that moment of relaxation, or ball watching, the good attackers will get an advantage. Always be aware, even while the opponent is preparing for a throw-in, corner, or free kick.

GOOD VISION

Good players see so much; it seems they know what is happening behind them as well as in front of them. Using oral communication and always looking around you will help ensure that you are not surprised by your opponent. No surprises usually means no goals by the opponents.

SAFE AND SIMPLE

When playing defense, the first job is to stop the opponent, the second is to win the ball, and the third is to build an attack. Before you win the ball, know *what* your move will be when you receive it. The quicker you make the transition, especially indoors, the better. Be safe and efficient when you are near your own goal. Do not dribble and try fancy things; the risk of losing the ball is too great.

Square passes are parallel to the goal and move in an east to west or west to east direction. If intercepted, square passes put two or three of your teammates out of defensive position (**Figure 9-6**).

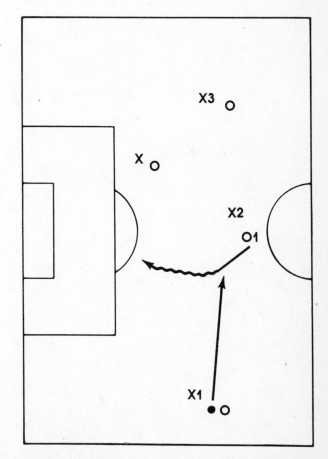

Figure 9-6. O1 steals a square pass, and X1, X2, and X3 are all displaced from good defensive position.

Keep possession of the ball. If you can play the ball forward, great; if not, keep possession. It is always better to pass back to your sweeper to retain possession than to lose the ball with an unstrategic forward pass. Often the sweeper or the goalkeeper is a player who is open to allow your team to keep possession. A pass to retain possession forces the opponent to adjust and can open up good forward passing options for your team. If you are under a lot of pressure and cannot find a safe option, then play the ball long.

TWO-ON-ONE

When a defender is caught in a two-on-one situation—two opponents with the ball approaching you, with all your teammates except the goalkeeper away from the play—you should position yourself between the ball and the opponent without the ball. This forces the player with the ball to make a move on you. You are making the play into an isolated one-on-one situation, and you are playing the highest percentage on winning the ball. And always try to force the player to the outside, giving him or her the worst angle for a shot.

10
OFFENSIVE PLAY

In Chapter 9 we said all players play defense. The converse is also true—all players play offense. The moment the ball is won from the opponent, all 11 players become attackers. Therefore, all players need to understand offensive play and what makes a successful offense.

Where you are on the field influences the types of risk you might want to take on offense. In Chapter 9 we recommended a safe and simple approach to defense and, above all, that you retain possession of the ball when you are near your own goal. You can become more adventurous (dribbling, making wall passes and difficult passes) as you advance up the field. In addition to these guidelines are some general principles that always apply to good offensive play.

PASSING

The weight, or pace, and accuracy of the pass are very important for success. In Chapter 3 we discussed different types of passes and exercises to work on. However, there is more to passing the ball than these fundamentals. Always pass the ball to the teammate in the direction he or she is moving. When passing to your teammate's feet, pass slightly to the side away from the defender *(Photo 10–1)*.

Passing and then coming to a stop is the quickest way for your team to lose the ball. Pass and move. The *give and go*, or wall pass, is based on passing and moving (**Figure 10-1**). Using the outside-of-foot pass is a deceptive way to set up the wall pass.

SUPPORTING YOUR TEAMMATES

Every time your team has the ball, every player should have two or three passing options. This happens only with support from other teammates.

Passing and moving are fundamental to the principle of support. As a teammate receives a pass, a couple of players should come toward him or her to provide support—but at least one or two players need to move away also. In this manner the player with the ball can make a short pass or a long pass (**Figure 10-2**).

The principle of support allows for combination plays. The wall pass, for example, was described earlier. Another play, the takeover, occurs when one player dribbles the ball and a supporting teammate takes the ball off the dribbler's foot and moves away in another direction (**Figure 10-3**).

Generally, you want to execute a takeover when you are moving parallel to the goal. As you dribble, screen the ball with your body while carrying the ball with the foot that is away from the defender. The teammate advancing toward you takes the ball away with the same foot. In Figure 10-3, X1 would be dribbling with his or her right foot and X2 would take the ball with his or her right foot. This method prevents collisions.

Another combination play is the overlap, which is a supporting run into the space your teammate has just opened (**Figure 10-4**). An overlapping run often is a curving run and creates many problems for defenders. The overlap is also a great weapon to get fullbacks involved in the attack.

MOVEMENT

All coaches require movement, but it is the type of movement that is important. Running at the same pace for a long time is not very effective in soccer. In order to lose the defender and support your teammate, you must be deceptive. A walk followed by a quick sprint has a better chance of getting you open than a fast jog.

Never wait for the ball. If you are receiving a pass, hold your ground, then come with speed to meet the ball. Work hard to get to the ball to make your next move.

Give the opponent a little misdirection. If you want to go to your left, take a step or two to the right before breaking back to the left. The run that uses misdirection will confuse the defender. In soccer we call this *checking runs* (**Figure 10-5**).

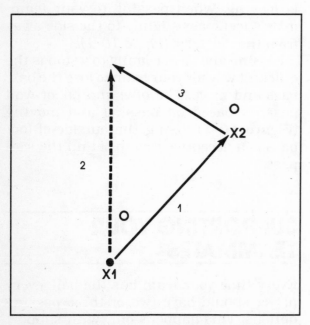

Figure 10-1. X1 passes to X2 and sprints for the return pass.

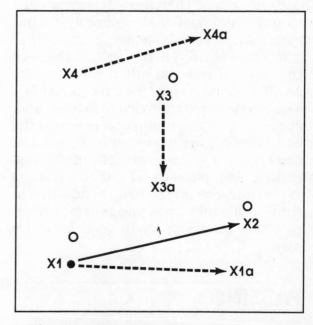

Figure 10-2. Notice how X1 and X3 come to supporting positions X1a and X3a, while X4 goes away to X4a. X2 now has three options, two short and one long.

Photo 10-1

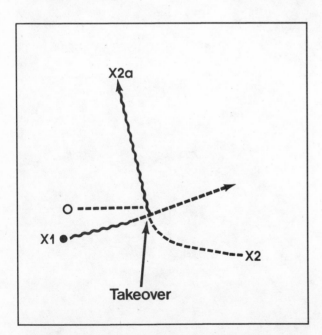

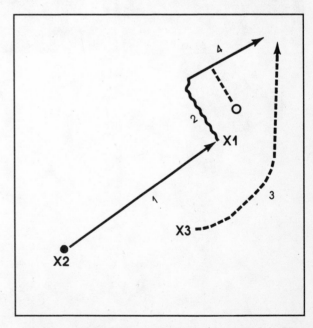

Figure 10-3. X1 dribbles the ball across the field. X2, coming from the opposite direction, takes the ball off his foot.

Figure 10-4. X1 receives a pass from X2 and dribbles the ball in at a diagonal, thereby opening up space for X3 to run into and receive the pass.

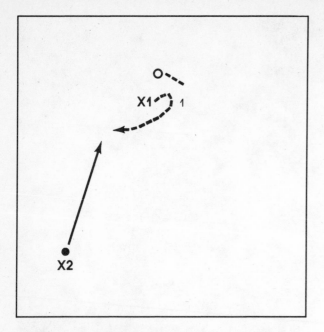

Figure 10-5. X1 moves in one direction, then in the opposite direction to receive the ball.

DRIBBLING

A key to good offense is getting a numerical advantage. This means you want to have more attackers than the other team has defenders. Professional teams are happy if they get even numbers.

Passing, supporting, and moving can all help create a numerical advantage through the give and go, overlap, deceptive run, and good pass techniques. The ability to burst, explode, and move quickly after you make a fake is the key to setting up a numerical advantage (10-2). A large opening is not always necessary. Forwards need to see a small opening and seize the advantage. Sometimes this might mean dribbling to the side to create an opening.

A successful dribbler can destroy any defense, as Maradona exemplifies per-

Photo 10-2

fectly. Beating an opponent by dribbling immediately puts your team at an advantage because you have one more attacker than the opposing team (**Figure 10-6**).

Whenever possible, try to dribble toward the attacking goal. Dribble to get past that first player, then get your head up. Now that your team has an advantage, it is your job to find the open player or continue dribbling if the opponent does not challenge you. Wall passes, overlaps, etc., become real options once you beat that first defender. Dribbling is a great option, especially in the attacking part of the field.

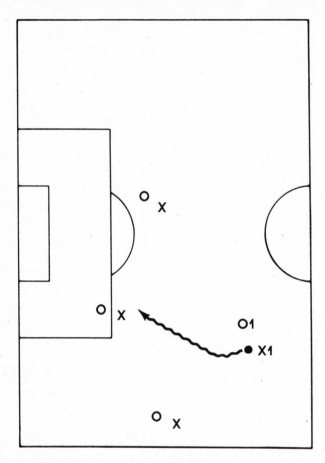

Figure 10-6. X1 dribbles past the defender, O1, thus creating a four-on-three opportunity for the Xs.

TOTAL AND SIMPLE

Soccer is a complete game, and to be a good player you must play the total game. Everyone should learn to play offense and defense. As a player, you spend most of the time without the ball; therefore, movement and support are very important. You must learn both of these skills to be a total player.

Soccer should be played simply. Good dribblers, like Maradona and Tatu, do not dribble to show off or do something fancy. They dribble because it is the simple option. What makes them great players is that their skill level is so high that everything *becomes* simple.

Being a good offensive player, then, means playing it simple, with the aim of helping your team score.

11

DEFENDERS

A defender's first job is to stop the opponent from scoring; the second job is to assist in his or her own team's attack. You are not a good defender if you only defend or if you attack before you have taken care of your defensive responsibility. Remember your priorities: defend first, attack second.

Defenders can be split into two groups; outside and inside defenders. The outside defender generally has good speed and stamina and joins the attack frequently in wide positions.

Inside, or central, defenders are generally bigger and are good headers of the ball. These defenders join the attack as additional midfielders and try to get on the end of cross balls.

General principles of good defense were discussed in Chapter 9. This chapter will go into more detail for defenders.

ZONE VERSUS MAN-TO-MAN

All defenders must be able to play zone or man-to-man defense. Many teams use a combination.

Man-to-man marking is really self-explanatory; the basic principles are explained in Chapter 9. A good exercise for your team is to play a game and give each player a direct opponent, with the restriction that you can defend only against that opponent. The result is a lot of one-on-one defense and determination.

Zone marking may be your team's style of defense; it *must* be used when the opposing team has the numerical advantage. As with man-to-man marking, playing between your goal and your opponent is very important. If the opponent is attacking three against two, the two defenders are more concerned with protecting the space, or zone, than the man. The principle of zone defense is to force the ball away from spaces that you want to protect. A zone defense also can allow you to double-team the ball while the rest of your team plays zone. The defensive team on an indoor power play is a good example of zone defense.

A good zone requires delay and support. The initial delay slows the opponent's momentum and allows your teammates to get on the goal side of the ball (**Figure 11-1**).

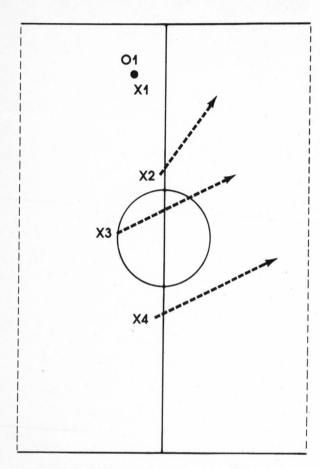

Figure 11-1. X1 delays O1, allowing X2, X3, and X4 to get behind the ball.

Notice in **Figure 11-1** that the players are getting into supporting positions. When the initial defender forces the attacker into the supporting defender, a double-team defense is created.

Where the supporting defender is positioned depends on what area of the field the ball is in; for example, if you as initial defender are relatively close to the goal, there is less space to choose from. The supporting defender's position also depends on the opponent's strengths, such as speed and dribbling ability.

A good exercise for teaching zone principles is to have defenders play at a numerical disadvantage (three-on-two, four-on-three, or six-on-four) until offense scores a goal or until defense takes possession. These exercises can be played to a goal or in a grid, with the object being to retain possession. Remember, the defenders in a numbers-down situation cannot stop the attackers forever; the coach hopes the defenders will make the attackers' job as difficult and time-consuming as possible. Forcing the attack to slow down allows teammates to recover.

HIGH PRESSURE VERSUS LOW PRESSURE

In addition to deciding between zone and man-to-man defense, the team and coach must decide on either high-pressure or low-pressure defense. But first, let's correct a common misconception: that zone defense and low-pressure defense are one and the same. They are not the same; zone can be used in either high- or low-pressure situations. The decision to use high- or low-pressure defense depends on the time of the game, the score, the area of the field, and the ability of the opponent.

For example, when playing a highly skilled opponent a defender might use a low-pressure defense in the first two-thirds of the field, allowing the opponent time and space until the players reach the defensive third. At that point, having saved his energy to concentrate his defensive efforts nearer his own goal, the defender will tighten up on the opponent.

Playing a team that is not very skilled calls for high-pressure defense. Put pressure on the opponent as early as possible to force a mistake. A defender using high pressure should play tight to the opponent whenever the ball is within playing distance. When the ball is on the far side of the field not in playing distance, it is not

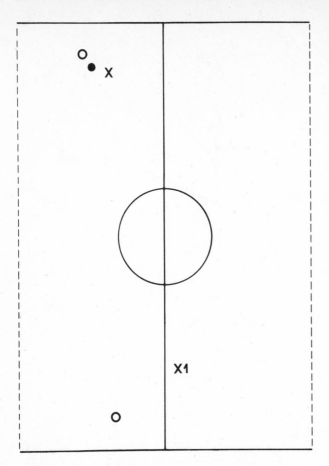

Figure 11-2. Defender X1 plays off the opponent when the ball is on the far side.

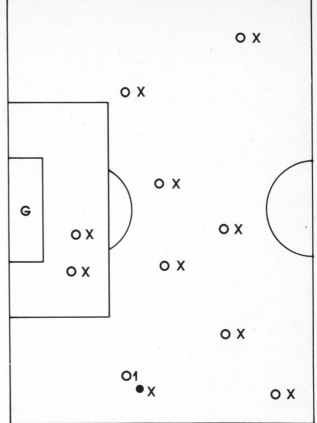

Figure 11-3. Incorrect concentration. O1 is exposed. There is no defensive concentration around the ball.

necessary to mark your opponent as tightly. This is to leave plenty of "cushion" to support your other teammates (**Figure 11-2**).

A good exercise is to play "conditioned" games, in which you regulate the way the game is played. An example is eight-on-eight, with one team playing high- or low-pressure defense.

CONCENTRATION

Defenders feel a lot more comfortable with other players around. Having teammates near means support and crowded spaces; therefore, the forward's job becomes difficult. Concentrating defenders near the ball gives you confidence to take a calculated risk to win the ball because you have support (**Figures 11-3 and 11-4**).

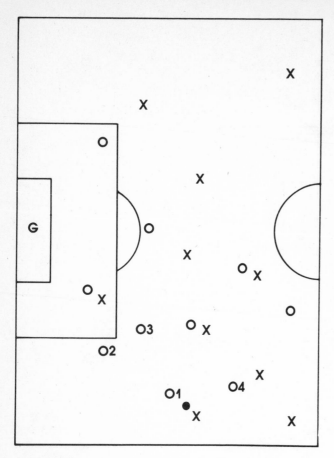

Figure 11-4. Correct concentration. Much better concentration on the ball due to support especially of O2, O3, and O4.

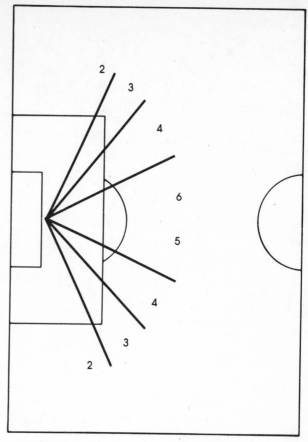

Figure 11-5. This figure shows the number of players to compose the defensive wall for free kicks taken from that area.

As an individual defender, you can play better if your team concentrates around the ball. A good exercise is to play seven-on-five to one big goal. The team of five plus goalkeeper is trying to possess the ball only. The team of seven is trying to exert pressure (concentrate), win the ball, and score. See how many goals you can score in five minutes.

DEFENSE AGAINST FREE KICKS

Defenders generally are nearer the goal, so as a defender you must organize quickly to take away the opponent's quick free kick. As mentioned in Chapter 14, the goalkeeper determines how many players are to be in the wall (**Figure 11-5**).

A forward should set up the wall from behind the ball. If the goalkeeper goes to the post to set up the wall, a quick free kick can be made easily.

The tallest defender (usually a central defender) is the first player in the wall,

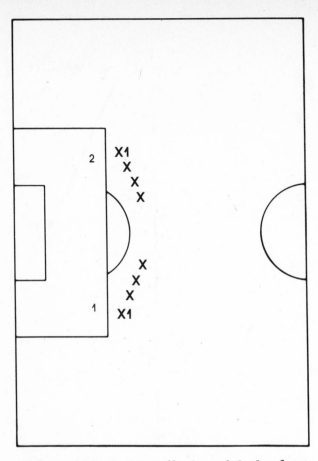

Figure 11-6. In walls 1 and 2 the first player is X1.

closest to the sideline (**Figure 11-6**). The remainder of the wall should be made up of midfielders and forwards. Defenders are the best markers, so except for the first player, they should be left out of the wall to mark the opponents. The key to a good wall is not to move; stay together. One player should be designated to attack the ball. This player is generally the inside player.

DEFENSE AGAINST CORNER KICKS

Once again, organizing quickly is important. Goalkeepers like to see a teammate at both the near and far posts. These players should be midfielders or forwards. Your best jumpers should mark the opponent's best jumpers. They must leave the post as the ball is cleared. This is important as it forces your opposition to retreat to an on-side position.

Remember, do not ball-watch. Run with your opponent and mark him or her in a goalside position.

TRANSITIONS

Once the defense wins the ball, the defenders must switch to offense as quickly as possible. A successful transition requires vision and concentration. Every defender should have an idea of what he or she wants to do with the ball before getting it. Quick decision making results in more goal-scoring opportunities.

Outside defenders want to get wide or move to the outside as quickly as possible. Central defenders should split their line—one player advancing back toward the goal, the other moving upfield 10 or 15 yards. Try to play the ball to the farthest open man as soon as possible. This player has the most space from which to start an attack. Passing the ball out of the back is preferred because it is faster than dribbling and less risky when you are close to your own goal.

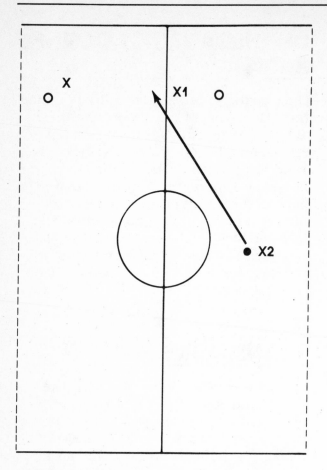

Figure 11-7. Incorrect offense. X1 is ahead of the ball as X2 wants to play it. This could result in X1 having to wait for the ball and reduces the space available to drive into.

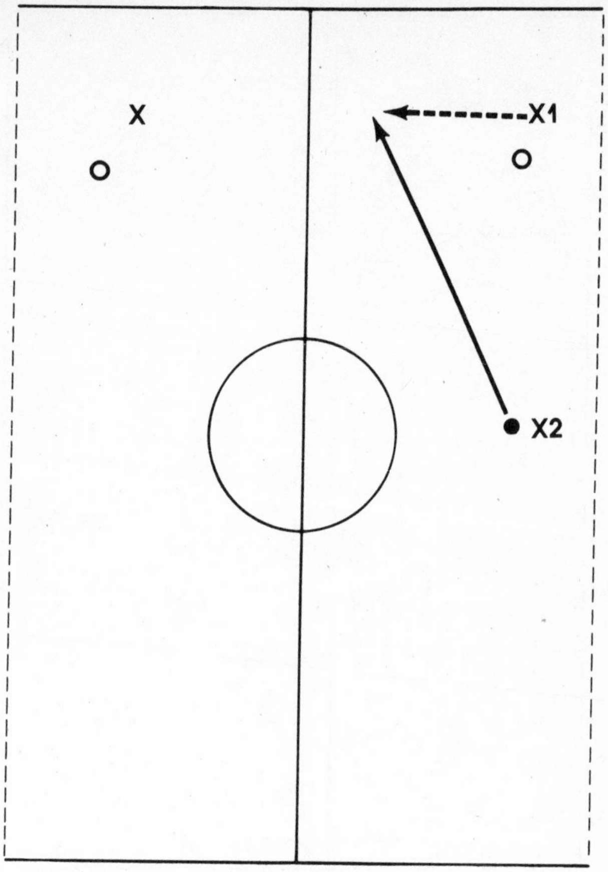

Figure 11-8. Correct offense. In this example, X1 is deeper and is moving into the space to receive the pass; he or she has more space to attack into.

DEFENDERS ON OFFENSE

Again, transition requires defenders to become offensive players quickly, and playing offense is an ability all good defenders must have. Forwards are often lazy defenders and do not like to chase, so a defender who can attack will be able to exploit this weakness (**Figures 11-7 and 11-8**).

12

MIDFIELDERS

The midfield can best be described as the engine room of the team. Here attacks are prepared and defense is initiated. Midfielders are diverse players who need to possess traits of both defenders and forwards.

In this chapter we will talk about the specific needs of a midfielder. However, the chapters dealing with defenders and forwards must also be looked at to get the complete picture of a midfielder's role.

PASSING AND VISION

Passing the ball to the best-positioned teammate requires technique and vision. A good midfielder must be able to chip passes over defenders, drive the ball through a narrow opening to a teammate, and curve the ball around defenders. Accuracy, pace, and technique result in good passes.

The ability to find well-positioned teammates is called *vision*. To have the greatest vision, a player should keep as much of the action in front of him as possible. Peripheral vision is important. You must also have the necessary fundamental skills. If your skills are poor, you will have to concentrate on the ball too much to keep your head up and look for teammates. Good vision also requires that you believe your eyes. The opening may be there for only a second or two; if you second-guess yourself or take another look, the opportunity will be gone. Trust your eyes and make the pass. Looking again and again makes a midfielder conservative and predictable. The midfielder's pass is important because it so strongly dictates what will happen in the play that immediately follows. Because a pass should be played away from the side of the defender, a well-executed pass will tell your teammate which way to turn. Passing, in fact, is the key to turning.

The following are some good exercises for midfielders.

- See **Figure 12-1**. The midfielder, X1, with his or her back toward the goal the team is attacking, receives the ball from the coach (C). As the pass is played, the coach calls out a number, which represents one of the forwards (O). This player makes a diagonal run; the midfielder must receive the ball and on the second or third touch, hit an accurate pass to the forward. After 8–10 passes, change the midfielder.

- See **Figure 12-2**. Using two balls, form a group of four and designate one midfielder (X). O1 and O2 each have a ball, and O3 does not. The midfielder, playing two-touch, must hit passes to the player without the ball. O1 passes to X; O3 is moving without the ball. X controls and passes to O3. Immediately, O2 passes to X, and O1 is moving without the ball. X controls and passes to O1, and so on.

- Play an eight-on-eight game to two big or small goals. One player on each team is designated as the midfielder,

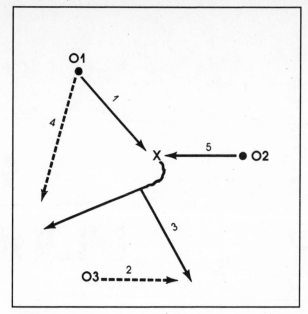

Figure 12-2

and every third pass must go to that player. This forces the midfielder to get open and gives the player repeated gamelike passing situations in a short time. After a time period of five minutes, pick another midfielder for each team.

SHOOTING

A midfielder in soccer is like a guard in basketball. If a midfielder can shoot the ball accurately, he or she will draw the defense out, thereby creating openings inside. A soccer midfielder plays on the perimeter of the offense, so shooting is vital.

Once again, good technique is a key to an accurate shot. But a midfielder often shoots from a distance, so power is also important. Effective power shooting is achieved by getting your whole body weight into the shot. As you explode into the ball, your velocity will result in your standing leg leaving the ground at the time of impact with the ball *(Photo 12–1)*.

Midfielders are often on the end of wall passes and give-and-go combinations, resulting in chances to score goals. The ability to shoot and score separates great midfielders from good midfielders.

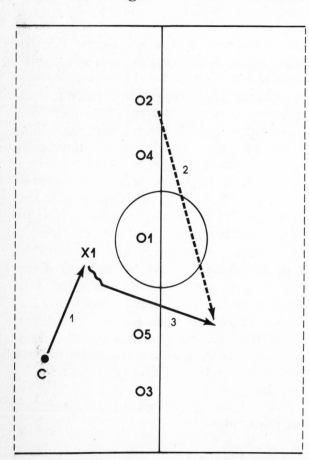

Figure 12-1

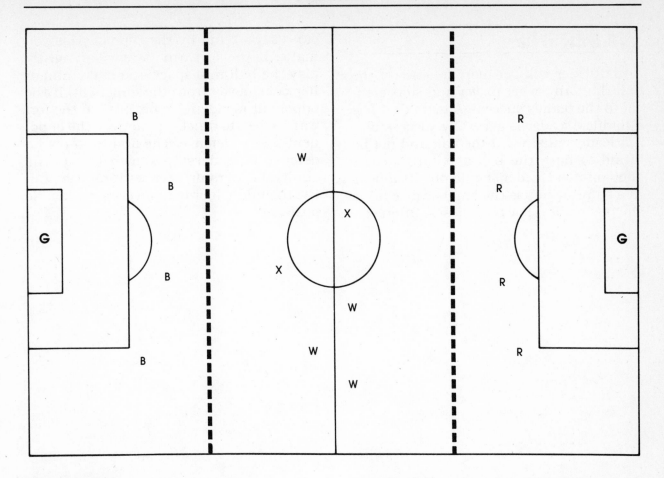

STAMINA

Midfielders do the most running during a game. They cover from the edge of one penalty box to the edge of the other. Sometimes they jog, other times they walk, and many times they sprint. But rarely do they stand still.

Fitness is important to a good midfielder. Only if you are fit can you execute passes and shoot accurately in the latter stages of a game. **Figure 12-3** shows a good exercise for midfield stamina.

Figure 12-3. The four whites (W) attack the four reds (R). The two midfielders (X) play with the Ws. The blues (B) are resting. The attackers are really playing six-on-four. When the reds win the ball, they try to break out of their defensive third against the six attackers (4W, 2X). If they are successful, the two midfielders (X) join the reds and attack the blues. The whites are now resting. By always playing with the offense the midfielders receive a good workout. After five minutes, pick two new midfielders.

LEADERSHIP

A midfielder will get more touches of the ball than any other player and so is critical to the team's success. A team that has a midfield leader is generally successful.

A leader must want the ball and not be afraid to have the ball at vital times. A good midfield leader should not disappear in a game or refuse the ball because he or she has made a few bad passes. Often you can lead a team by the type of pass you make. If the forward is marked tightly, play the ball into space and make him or her come away from the opponent. If the opponent is playing zone, pass to the forward's feet, to quickly penetrate the opponent's zone defense. The ability to read a defense is leadership shown in passing ability. Leadership goes with responsibility; the midfielder is in a very responsible position.

13

FORWARDS

Being quick, fast, strong, dynamic, and unpredictable are all key to being a great forward. Taking full advantage of the openings and weaknesses of the defense is also important. The ability to score goals can make you an overnight hero *(Photo 13–1)*. Forwards are allowed to be soccer's greatest risk takers. While a certain level of confidence is allowed, you must always be aware of your teammates' positions. A strong belief in your skills is important to you if you intend to be a successful attacker. As a forward, you need to push yourself, but at the same time have patience. You must be hungry for the ball and always look to finish (put the ball in the goal). You should have the same attitude in practice so scorning becomes second nature.

Principles of good offensive play were discussed earlier. In this chapter we will characterize the specific abilities a good forward needs.

SHIELDING

Better players and better teams often can take away the space that a forward has available to run into. With young players, the ball is kicked through to the forward, who then runs it down. As you get older, those spaces are more difficult to find; therefore, a forward receives a lot of passes with his or her back to the goal. Shielding the ball is vital to a forward's success. Shielding is the art of placing your body between the opponent and the ball. The ball must always be within playing distance *(13–2)*.

A good beginning exercise is to have one player hold the ball with both hands while an opponent tries to slap the ball. After players can do this, the same principle is used, except the ball is on the ground and no hands are used. A player must lean back to shield the ball properly and get sufficient space to drop back a pass or turn on the defender. It is easier when you can feel the defender with your body, because you can tell whenever the defender moves and then react appropriately *(13–3 and 13–4)*.

Many players use the sole of their foot when shielding. Use your *toe*, not the sole.

Photo 13-1

Photo 13-2

By using the toe you will not be as heavy on the ball and will be able to change direction quickly.

Shielding comes into play when a forward is marked tightly. Never wait on the pass when marked tightly; always come to the ball. If the defender hesitates, you have space; if the defender comes with you, use your ability to shield the ball.

The purpose of protecting the ball is to retain possession. Shielding is used to turn past a defender by getting the defender to lean one way while you turn in the other direction.

Photo 13-3

Photo 13-4

DRIBBLING, HEADING, AND SHOOTING

Good forwards are good dribblers. A one-on-one situation should be an advantage for your team if your forward is a good dribbler. The abilities to change pace, stop quickly, and feint were discussed in Chapter 5.

In outdoor soccer many goals are scored with the head. The ability to time high balls properly and the courage to head the ball with a goalkeeper and defenders bearing down on you are attributes of a good forward. Heading technique was discussed in Chapter 7.

A forward must possess all kinds of shooting techniques. Using both feet is important because close to the goal the opponent will not give you time to set up your good foot. Coaches should remember that forwards score goals from the inside of the penalty box and mostly between the goal box and the penalty spot, so forwards should practice shooting there. A quick release is the key to scoring goals. A surprised goalkeeper does not have time to set and dive.

Shooting technique was discussed in Chapter 6.

SPEED AND QUICKNESS

A combination of speed and quickness in a player is a coach's dream.

Speed is the ability to run fast over a distance. In soccer, forwards are usually called upon to run a sprint of 10–40 yards in a game.

Quickness is the ability to react, change direction, and take only a step or two to get into high gear. Many forwards have either speed or quickness; the really great forwards, like Maradona of Argentina, have both.

The speed and quickness of a defender also influence a forward's play. Take a slow defender away from the goal so you have room to use your speed to beat him or her. Stay close to the goal when playing against fast defenders; that way you neutralize their speed advantage.

Unpredictability

The battle between a good forward and a good defender is both a physical and a mental one. As a forward, you have the advantage of knowing what you want to do. The defender is usually forced to react. A defender who "bites," or goes into a tackle, early is easily beaten. Reacting to a defender's mistake is ideal for a forward. Initially, be patient and wait for that mistake. If it is not forthcoming, then you must surprise your opponent.

The mental part of the game requires deception. In order to beat a defender, sometimes you should do the obvious. At other times you should fake one way and then go the other. Find out which is the defender's weak side and go at that side. But whatever you do, never be predictable. If the defenders figure you out, they will stop you. Deceive them; every time defenders think they can read you, change and keep them guessing.

In order to be unpredictable you must be a good technical player. Good technique allows you to go to your left or right, shoot or pass with either foot, and use any part of your body to control the ball. Be creative and innovative—but never predictable.

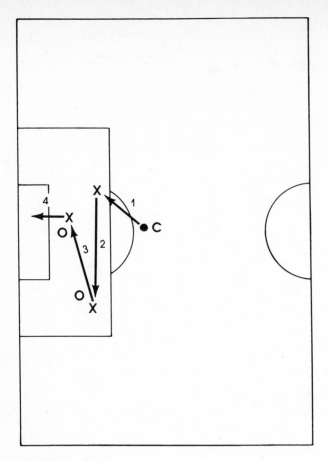

Figure 13-1. Three attackers (X) versus two or three defenders (O) in the penalty box. The coach serves the balls from outside the penalty box. The forwards must make two or three passes before they can shoot. This restriction forces movement (on and off the ball), dribbling, shielding, and the eventual shot. The shooting takes place in the penalty box, which is how it happens in the game itself.

MOVEMENT

Scoring goals requires that a forward gain sufficient space to get the shot off. Sometimes speed, quickness, dribbling, or a good pass can give you that space. Most of the time the ability to play without the ball and to stay constantly on the move when near the opponent's goal gives the forward the necessary space.

Every time the defender who is marking looks away, a good forward moves to a new position. By constantly moving, you make defenders nervous, especially when you are near the goal. The more active you are, the less the defender wants to look away from you. As the defender concentrates on you, he or she will eventually get out of position with relation to the ball and will be in poor marking position. Now an effective run by the forward will get him or her open for a shot on goal.

Figure 13-1 shows a good exercise to combine many elements of forward play.

14

GOALKEEPER

The goalkeeper is the last line of defense and the first part of the attack. He or she is integral to the success of your team. The goalie can make up for mistakes in front of him or her and can get an assist on offense, especially in indoor soccer. A goalkeeper, however, does not have the same luxury as the rest of the players. When a goalkeeper makes a mistake, 90 percent of the time the end result is a goal scored.

Often players and coaches neglect the goalkeeper because he or she is a specialist. The goalkeeper requires different training, is the only player that can use his or her hands, and has to be courageous almost to a fault.

Being a goalkeeper is often a very lonely job. However, great teams have great goalkeepers. What makes a goalkeeper successful? What skills must a good goalie possess?

SHOT BLOCKING

A good goalkeeper must save shots. Mistakes are going to be made, and the result will be a shot on goal, which the team will expect the goalkeeper to save. Making saves requires the ability to catch, dive, jump, punch, and play the angles.

Catching

The general technique for catching is the "W" method (Photo 14–1). This method is used primarily for shots above the waist. Remember, you want to catch with your hands and not with your body.

Catching balls below the waist or bouncing balls requires a "scoop" or "shovel" technique. Bring your elbows in, hands down, and "scoop" the ball into your chest. (14–2).

Photo 14-1

You can collect rolling balls in two ways: the straight-leg pickup *(14–3)* and the bent knee behind the ball *(14–4)*.

In the bent knee pickup, the shoulders remain square with the field of play. Your body is behind the ball in both methods in case the ball slips through your hands.

The outdoor goalkeeper must also deal with many cross balls (long, lofted passes from wing positions into the penalty area) per game. Catching crosses is based on

Photo 14-2

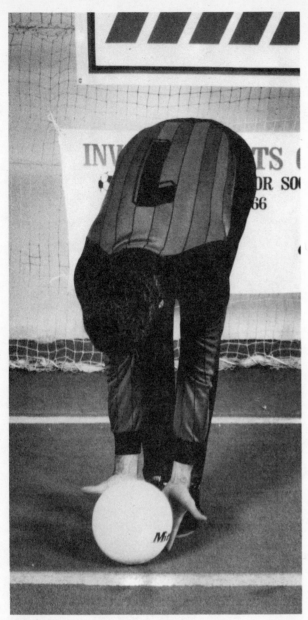

Photo 14-3

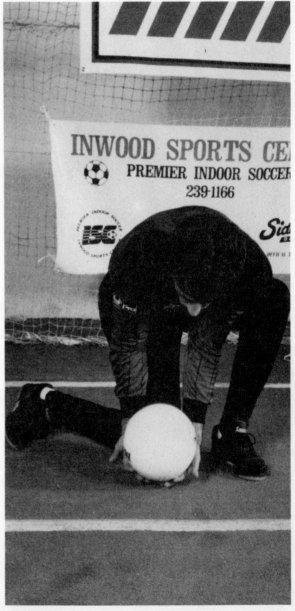

Photo 14-4

Photo 14-5

Photo 14-6

the "W" technique, with an emphasis on catching the ball at the highest point possible. Driving off one leg when jumping will give you more height *(14–5 and 14–6)*. Catching the ball at its highest point gives the goalkeeper the advantage over an attacking player who tries to head the ball.

Punching

When punching, the goalkeeper can use either a one-handed or a two-handed punch. The one-handed punch is used to continue the path of the ball, while slightly altering its direction and altitude. The one-handed punch should be a short, brisk strike with the fist *(14–7)*. The two-handed punch should be used either to send the ball back where it came from or to change its direction. Whether using the one-handed or two-handed punch, it is important to redirect the ball toward the sideline and out of a dangerous scoring angle.

Diving

Diving to make a save makes for some of soccer's best pictures *(14–8)*. Learning to land, however, is one of the most difficult arts. Notice that we addressed catching before diving. Once a goalkeeper has mastered catching, he or she can fully concen-

Photo 14-7

Photo 14-8

Photo 14-9   **Photo 14-10**

Photo 14-11

Photo 14-12

trate on diving. A good progression, from simple to complex, is the key to learning how to dive.

The first stage is to learn from a kneeling position. Learn how to roll off your hips and not land on your elbows (*14–9 to 14–12*).

Next, practice in a standing position with a dive. When diving, it is important to bend at the waist and keep the lower hand in line with the ball. The upper hand should be on top of the ball for control, with the ground as the third surface to catch with if necessary (*14–13 to 14–16*).

The crossover step or side step comes after success at the standing position. The side step is a slight, sideways skip, the feet moving from left to right or right to left, depending on the direction of the dive. The crossover step crosses the left foot over the right to move to the right, or the right over the left to move in the left direction.

In initial exercises, the coach should let the goalkeeper know in which direction he or she is supposed to dive. When the goalkeeper understands diving, then a random sequence of shots can be used to practice.

Photo 14-13

Photo 14-14

Photo 14-15

Photo 14-16

Angles

Positioning, or angle play, is the bread and butter of good goalkeepers. Young goalies are always making spectacular diving saves, while it appears that veteran goalkeepers get all shots aimed straight at them. A goalkeeper, whether on his line or coming out on a breakaway, must always know where he is in relation to the net. Good positioning takes experience and young players should be patient.

A helpful hint to explain angles (short corners, long corners) is to use a rope about 50 feet long and tie an end around each post. Put your goalkeeper's leg in the middle and move the ball around the goal in an arc so he can see firsthand how the angles change.

Using angles makes the goal as small as possible for attacking players. Remember, good goalkeepers are not glued to the goal line. The goalkeeper can use an arc as a guideline for angle play (**Figure 11-1**).

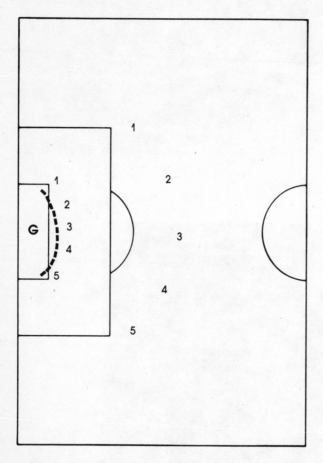

Figure 14-1. As illustrated in the diagram below, the goalkeeper should follow the "arc" of defense, according to where the ball is in play. For instance, if the ball is located at #3 on the field, the goalkeeper should be in position 3 in the box. As you can see, the positions 1–5 relate to each other. The wider the ball is, generally the closer the goalkeeper is to the post.

DISTRIBUTION

Once the save has been made, the goalkeeper starts the attack. How the goalie does so—which teammate he gives the ball to and how—is called *distribution* in soccer. The initial outlet for the ball is key to a team's ability to counterattack, especially indoors.

A good rule for goalies to follow is to first check the opposite side of play. Often the offense has overloaded one side of the field, and by distributing to the far side, the counterattack can start with little or no pressure.

A goalie who is mentally playing all phases of the game will know which method of distribution will be effective in which circumstances and will help greatly in developing a team's attack.

The type of distribution used depends on the distance from goalie to teammate and on the individual strengths of the goalkeeper. The trademarks of a good distribution are that it is accurate, gets to the teammate quickly, and is easy to control.

Throwing

The overhand throw is quick and powerful. This method of distribution is vital for an indoor goalie (*14–17 and 14–18*). David Vanole (UCLA) of the 1988 U.S. Olympic team has a fine overhand throw that is accurate and can cover a great distance.

The underhand, or bowling, throw is used for short distances. Being on the ground, this throw is easy for players to control (*14–19*).

Photo 14-17

Photo 14-18

Photo 14-19

Punting

The volley punt is used most often. Generally, this type of kick is high but fairly accurate. A volley occurs when the ball is punted directly out of the hands without hitting the ground.

The half-volley has a lower clearance, but generally more distance, than the volley. A half-volley occurs when the ball is struck just after it rebounds up from the ground after having been dropped from the hands *(14–20 and 14–21)*.

Photo 14-21

Photo 14-20

ORGANIZATION

The goalkeeper is the one player who almost always has the play in front of him or her, so the goalie sees more of the game than any other player. If you're a goalkeeper, organizing your defense can spare you a lot of work. It's obvious, therefore, that communication and leadership are important traits for a goalkeeper. The goalie's instructions should be clear and concise so that the maximum is achieved with a minimum of talking.

It's vital that the goalie organize the defense for corner kicks and free kicks. When the team wants to avoid a quick free kick, a field player should set up the wall, but it's the goalie who determines how many players make up the wall. The number of players that make up the wall is determined by the danger of the free kick.

CONCENTRATION

A good team can sustain an attack for many minutes, especially in an outdoor game. The goalkeeper might have very little to do for 10–15 minutes and then suddenly be faced with a counterattack. Can the goalie make the save?

Being able to concentrate even when inactive is a trait you need to learn if you hope to become a good goalkeeper. Indeed, in professional soccer, the ability to make a big save after being inactive is what separates the great goalkeepers from the good ones. Playing the game in your mind when your team is on the attack often allows you to stay mentally in the game.

To keep your mind on the game, put yourself in the shoes of your teammates and opponents and anticipate every action. Sometimes mentally narrating the game, play-by-play, will help you keep your mind on the field rather than concentrating on play only when the ball is in your immediate space.

If you're a goalkeeper, follow the same play pattern as your team. When the ball is near the opponent's goal, position yourself near the top of your penalty box. As the ball approaches midfield, you should be 7–8 yards from your goal line. Moving in this pattern will help your mental play so that you will not be surprised by the opponent.

SPECIAL SITUATIONS

1. On corner kicks the goalie should be approximately three to four yards from the near post. He or she should position defenders to cover both the near and far posts.
2. A penalty kick is a difficult situation. Having seen the kicker take one before can help you anticipate. If the player shoots very hard, it is often best to step forward and give up the corners. If the player places the shot, guessing one side is often your best chance. Either way, the shooter is in control of the situation and the goalie can only hope to capitalize on the shooter's mistakes.
3. A breakaway occurs when an offensive player has beaten the defense and is attacking the goal in a one-on-one confrontation with the goalkeeper. A breakaway requires that the goalkeeper understand angles. Move out quickly but with control once you feel none of your defenders will stop the attacker. Every time the attacker touches the ball, you should be set and balanced; move forward only when the attacker is running after the ball. Do not go down too early, and when you do dive, cover as much of the goal as possible.

Experience is what makes a goalkeeper good. Play a lot of games, face a lot of shots and crosses, and each day you will become better able to anticipate. But there is more to being a good goalkeeper than stopping shots. Organization, communication, good distribution, and leadership combine to make a good goalkeeper.

15

SPECIFIC FUNDAMENTALS FOR INDOOR SOCCER

The game of soccer requires the same fundamentals and the same basic tactics whether it's played outdoors or indoors. The difference lies in emphasis. Certain talents and skills must be stronger for indoor soccer; others must be stronger to play outdoor soccer. Additionally, the size of the field, the number of players, the method of substitution, and other rules dictate some differences in tactics between the indoor and outdoor games.

TALENT AND TECHNIQUE

- Due to the field size, short, tight passing skills are at a premium in indoor soccer. A good indoor player needs to make quick passing decisions, and because long passes are not allowed to be struck in the air over three lines, passes generally must be made to the feet of the player's teammate.
- Tight passing in turn requires tight trapping skills. The opponent is

closer, the field is smaller, and therefore a player's ability to cushion the ball well is vital.
- Dribbling can destroy an indoor defense just as it can an outdoor defense. The indoor game requires a dribbler with great quickness, though speed is less important than in the outdoor game because of the smaller space.
- You don't need to be as good a header in the indoor game. Heading is not vital indoors because there are few long chip passes.
- How quickly can you get your shot off? That's the key question for an indoor player. Time is short, and space is limited. Every shot is a high-percentage rebound opportunity. An indoor forward always has to be on the prowl and ready to release a shot.
- Forwards have to be especially quick, with good turning ability and shielding skills.

A good shooting exercise is shown in **Figure 15-1**.

117

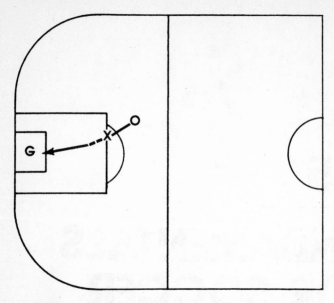

Figure 15-1. X has his or her back to the goal and is about 12 yards out with legs apart. O plays a ball at an angle through X's legs. X turns and tries to shoot immediately without taking more than one step. After 10–15 shots, change roles. This exercise can be done from different positions on the field, as well as different start positions for the shooting players.

STRATEGY AND TACTICS

Defense

- Good defensive tactics are similar for indoor with a few exceptions. There are more one-on-one situations, and because of the three-line pass rule, a defender can front-mark the attacker at times (**Figure 15-2**).
- Man-to-man marking is almost always employed when the opponent is within your own red line. Pressure is generally dictated by the point man (the center forward). If the center forward pressures, the whole team must play high-pressure defense.
- If you are the only player between the ball and your goalkeeper, play conservatively; never use fancy passes or dribbling.
- A good defensive player does not let the forward know where he is.
- Playing goalkeeper is much different indoors from outdoors. The many shots and rebounds, the close proximity of the fans, and the field size all make an indoor goalkeeper's job both interesting and nerve-racking. Additionally, the size of the playing surface and the three-line rule make for very few cross balls.
- In general, an indoor goalkeeper wants to stay on his or her feet more because shots wide of the goal become rebounds off the boards. Being able to "read" the boards is vital to the goalkeeper's success.
- A strong, accurately thrown distribution leads to assists. The goalkeeper who can play with his or her feet like a field player is an invaluable asset indoors.
- Because the goal is smaller, the crossover or side step prior to diving is not used as often indoors.
- Line changes can destroy a team if done at the wrong time. You should change only if your team has possession. Remember, sprint off; don't jog.

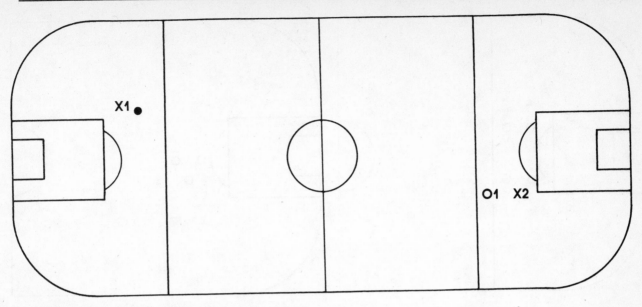

Figure 15-2. Defender O1 can mark striker X2 from the front side because X1 cannot play the ball over O1's head due to the three-line rule.

When you come on as a fresh defender, try to go to the far side of the field; that way your defensive partner is nearer the bench, and it will be easier to change. Also, watch the player you are changing with. Sometimes the game will dictate that a switch be made after only 20–30 seconds. Don't be at the water cooler when your partner needs a change.

- Power-play defense requires hard work, defensive concentration, and mental discipline from all four defenders. Two basic types of systems are used (**Figures 15-3 and 15-4**).

- Basic systems require zone marking and shifting. The initial defender challenging the ball is trying to take away a passing option through his or her angle of approach. Taking away an option makes it easier for the players behind the initial defender to defend (**Figure 15-5**).

- All free kicks in indoor soccer are direct, so setting up quickly is essential to good defense. Combining free kicks, power-play defense, and field size means a good indoor defender blocks shots. Shot blocking is a skill and requires courage.

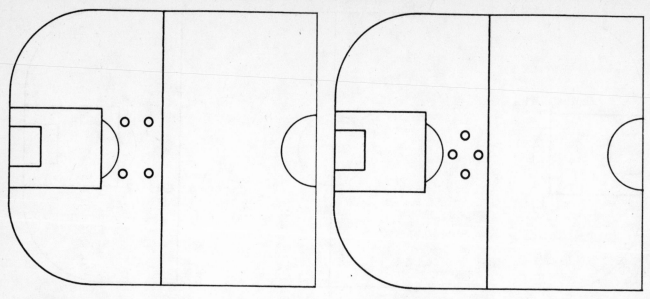

Figure 15-3. The square as a power-play defense.

Figure 15-4. The diamond as a power-play defense.

Offense

- Offensively, indoor soccer involves everyone. Goalkeepers can get assists, and many defenders are significant offensive players.
- The wall becomes another dribbling option for getting around the opponent.
- There is no offside rule, so players can position themselves deep in opposing territory and behind defenders.
- Pass and move is even more important in indoor soccer.
- Do not crowd the offensive zone. Stay spread out.
- Support from behind is essential in indoor soccer.
- The coach should keep most of the players behind the ball in order to lessen vulnerability to counterattack.

- Due to shifts played indoors, a forward faces many defenders. Study the defenders when you are not on the floor; you might spot a weakness you can exploit. Establish a style of play in your first two to three shifts and then change it. Try to remember what was successful for you and come back to it in the last quarter.
- Playing forward is not easy, but scoring a goal is a worthwhile reward for all the hard work.

Remember, soccer is soccer, whether outdoor or indoor. The emphasis is different, but the skills are the same.

- Once a goalkeeper picks up the ball and releases it, he or she cannot pick

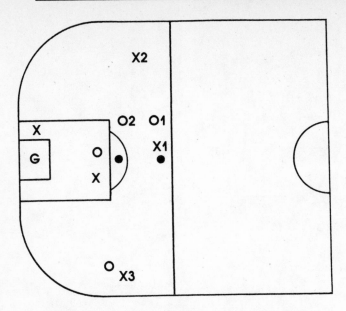

Figure 15-5. O1 approaches X1 at an angle to eliminate the pass to X2 and force the ball to X3. This allows O2 to come inside of X2.

it up until it is touched by the opposing team. Therefore, using high pressure can be a great offensive tactic.

- You can never relax on offense, because rebounds off the boards and/or goalkeepers are so frequent.

16

SOCCER REQUIREMENTS

Soccer is an active sport. In order to play it well you must take care of yourself. You take care of your car so you can get from place to place. As a soccer player you must take care of your body so you can perform.

Understanding tactics and being able to execute technique properly are useless if you are physically unfit. To become and stay fit you need to give your body the proper fuel—nutritious food. Finally, you need the right equipment to execute your soccer skills.

FITNESS

Young players should be fairly active, playing during recess at school and with friends after school. Fitness should not be the sole function of practice for young players, however, since there is already an element of fitness in the regular practice activities. Specific fitness should begin with players only in their teens; but again, it should be incorporated into regular practice as much as possible.

Just as important as fitness is flexibility. Stretching should be a part of warm-up, as well as cool-down, for older players. Remember not to stretch without first warming up the body with light jogging, relaxed dribbling, and the like.

A soccer player needs to be fit in three areas: aerobic (general endurance), anaerobic (interval training), and speed (full recovery, short sprints). A coach needs to change the routine to prevent fitness training from becoming a chore. Incorporating the ball into fitness training is critical because it helps improve or maintain a player's skills. Remember that young players (ages 5–12) get their fitness from the normal practice routine and their own high-energy activity levels.

Endurance

The foundation of fitness is general endurance. Running a distance of three to five miles two or three times a week for players from 14 to retirement is a solid way to build and maintain general endurance. When possible, a coach would like the team to achieve general fitness prior to the start of the season. That way, practice can enhance general endurance, not concentrate on it.

Interval Training

A player is required to sprint, then walk or jog, and then sprint again in games. Often, when the second sprint comes, the player has not recovered fully from the first sprint. This soccer fitness requirement can be trained by using an interval method. Initially, a coach should begin with a 3:1 rest-to-work ratio. The goal is to train eventually at a 1:1 ratio.

Interval training can be specific to fitness. Some examples of exercises include:

- A 40-yard sprint (5–7 seconds) followed by a rest period (15–20 seconds). Then repeat. Do 10 sets.
- Sit-ups for 30 seconds. Rest for 1 minute and 30 seconds. Then repeat. Do 5 sets.

Both examples are 3:1 rest-to-work ratios and are pure fitness drills.

Interval training can be soccer-specific, as in **Figures 16-1 and 16-2**.

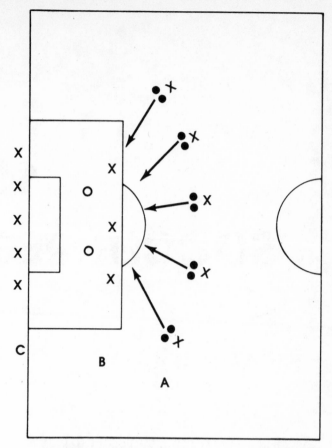

Figure 16-2. There are three groups of five, A, B, and C. Group A is serving balls to the working group B, while group C retrieves missed shots. Group B plays the three-on-two shooting game. After a work interval of one or two minutes the groups rotate. Once again, this is a 2:1 rest-to-work exercise.

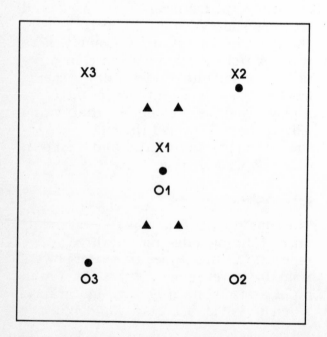

Figure 16-1. X1 plays one-on-one against O1. O2, O3, X2, and X3 have extra balls so that there is always a ball in play. After 45 seconds to a minute, X2 plays against O2 and so on. Notice this exercise is a 2:1 ratio.

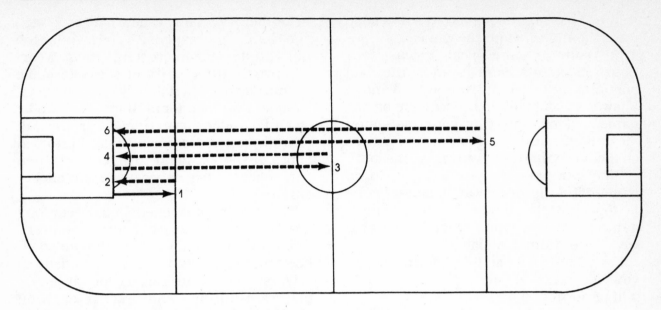

Figure 16-3. Run from the penalty box to the first line and back, then to the second, then to the third, then to the other penalty box and back. This is a hard workout, but it is excellent for indoor fitness.

As you can see by the examples, interval training and the fitness it enhances can be part of a regular soccer training program.

The game of indoor soccer can exemplify interval training at its best. Due to the field size and the nature of the game, shorter sprints need to be emphasized, and interval training should be a mainstay of practice. Running lines using the indoor field layout is a great conditioner (**Figure 16-3**).

Speed

An area often neglected for the older player is pure speed work. Interval training allows a recovery period, but this period is too short to allow complete recovery. When training for pure speed, the recovery should be complete. Generally,

this training should take place just after the warm-up so that the players are not fatigued.

NUTRITION

Food is the fuel our bodies use to perform. Good eating habits can enhance performance. The purpose of this section is to provide some commonsense guidelines. Parents are mainly responsible for their children's meals and therefore play a vital role in their nutrition.

Stay away from sodas, candy, and ice cream. Use juice and water to replenish the body's fluids. Water at halftime is readily accessible and quite good for your body.

The day before a game and the day of the game are important. The day before a game, carbohydrates are vital. A dinner that has pasta as its main course is a good meal the night before the game.

Eat your pregame meal at least four hours prior to kickoff to allow the food enough time to get into your system and to allow your stomach to concentrate on the game, not on digesting your just-eaten meal. Potassium is a good energy source so include bananas in your pregame meal.

Since you will perspire a lot during a game, drinking lots of water before a game is important. The intake of water prior to a game is critical when playing in warm weather or humid climates.

Use common sense to determine when you eat and what you eat, and your body will perform well for you.

EQUIPMENT

In earlier chapters we have talked about many techniques used by soccer players. Controlling a ball, shooting, passing, and dribbling all require you to have a good feel with your feet. Shoes that are oversized make it difficult for you to perform well.

It is better to buy inexpensive shoes that fit properly and buy a new pair each season than to buy expensive shoes a size too big so that you can grow into them. Wearing two or three pairs of socks to make oversized shoes fit will only cause blisters.

Shoes designed for artificial turf can be worn for indoor or artificial surfaces, although we recommend flat-bottomed shoes. If the artificial turf gets wet, then turf shoes are better because of the slicker surface.

The indoor goalkeeper should wear long goalkeeper pants to avoid burns from artificial turf. A goalie jersey with padded elbows and gloves is also recommended.

We suggest shin guards for all young players. Uniforms and practice clothing should be loose-fitting so you have freedom to move around. Wear the proper clothing to practice; it is tough to train wearing a pair of jeans and tennis shoes.

Soccer is a lifetime sport that you can enjoy as a youth, an adult, or a senior, as a recreational or competitive player. The enjoyment that the game gives you can be shared in so many ways. Soccer is a game with a million options, so have fun and never stop learning.

GETTING THE MOST OUT OF SOCCER

One of the questions we are most often asked by younger players is, "Do you think I can play college or professional soccer some day?" It's a question that you can answer better than anyone else. But we do know this—no matter which teams you play for, you can learn to enjoy the sport for life if you always aim to improve.

Many young players get to a skill level in soccer that puts them ahead of their teammates and they then become cocky and rest on their laurels. And before they know it, many others catch up to their level and they are left behind.

Soccer is a sport where there is always room for improvement. We have attained many of this country's top professional soccer honors, but what keeps us going is that we know that at every practice or game, we are going to learn something new about playing the sport.

Players need to remember that soccer is a team game. No soccer game was ever won by one player. (Put your team's best player on the field versus an opposing team and see how easily they score goals.) You will enjoy yourself and get along with your teammates only if you know the difference between confidence (OK) and selfishness (not OK).

Reading this book is only a start in improving your soccer skills. It will not make you a better player unless you practice what it says. And practice. And practice. And practice.

If you think about what you can get out of soccer—making yourself into a great athlete, learning about teamwork and sportsmanship, making new friends, and playing forever—this practice can lead to a lot of fun.

We're interested in your progress. Please let us know how your soccer is going and how we can help you better understand this great sport.

Tatu
850 Third Avenue
21st Floor
New York, NY 10022

Kevin Crow
4320 LaJolla Village Drive
Suite 300
San Diego, CA 92122

Pecorari, Antonio Carlos

Pecorari, Antonio Carlos